COMES THE
WHISPER

Take My Hand Child, Look in My Face

Laura Galvin

ISBN: 1500256412
ISBN 13: 9781500256418

I would like to dedicate this
to our precious Father God
whose love for us is beyond compare.

THANK YOU

I would like to thank all my friends and family for the help and encouragement they have given me. Kassie for the cover and Whitney for helping me design my book. And lastly, for my persistent grandson, Kyle, who continually bugged me. With love! What a blessing you have all been to me, I especially thank you for all your love and prayers.

Most of all thank You Father for using me, Your child, to write Your words of encouragement to all who read this book. Again I say, thank You Father! Thank You for loving me, thank You for using me in spite of myself. Thank You for sending Your Son to save me, thank you that I get to spend eternity with You!! Thank You, thank You, thank You!

Every time I think of you I give thanks to my God.
Philippians 1:3 NLT

COMES THE WHISPER

"Go out and stand before me on the mountain,"
the Lord told him.
And as Elijah stood there the Lord passed by,
and a mighty windstorm hit the mountain;
it was such a terrible blast that the rocks were torn loose,
but the Lord was not in the wind.
After the wind there was an earthquake,
but the Lord was not in the earthquake.
And after the earthquake, there was a fire,
but the Lord was not in the fire.
And after the fire
there was the sound of a gentle whisper.
When Elijah heard it, he wrapped his face in his scarf
and went out and stood at the entrance of the cave.
And a voice said, "why are you here Elijah?"
1st Kings 19:11-13 LB

Elijah was hiding in a cave (I think we could call it, a cave of depression, ever been there?) wishing he was dead, because things hadn't worked out as he thought they should have. He had already forgotten the mighty miracles God had done through him, he just wanted God to kill him and get it over with. (Please read Elijah's story and see how God used him in 1 Kings 18 & 19) He was tired and it seemed as he was the only one left that loved God, so what was the use. And like God told Elijah, He tells us, child most of the time it's not big exciting things, it's just everyday life. What you'll have is My still small whisper in your heart. Will that be enough for you? Will you keep on walking with Me, keep on letting Me use you, even when you feel like a failure? Will you please realize that you can't do this on your own, that you'll never be able to do it on your own! You must take my hand, look into My face, and see the love I have for you, and have always had for you. Let Me walk with you and guide you through your life, and then through eternity. Will you please trust Me to do this child?

So often that's where the Lord finds us, in the cave of failure, or disappointment, kicking ourselves. Thinking that we are useless to Him. But, let's think for a moment of, all of God's people, it seems like everyone of us, from the Bible times till now have blown it, in one way or another. Have sinned by being selfish, by being unloving, unkind, judgmental, immoral, or worse. We continually seem to forget the things He has taught us. Thank God! That all it takes is for us to give up justifying our sins, drop on our face in repentance, to ask His forgiveness, and be willing to receive it. To let Him turn our faces to His, so we can see the deep love He has for us. To let Him turn our ear to His whisper. To realize that His Spirit is in us! That He'll always be there to love us, to lead and guide us, and most of all to catch us when we fall, to pick us up dust us off and start us on His way again.

BIEN

My prayer is that as you read this book, it will help you to understand the great love your Father God has for you. The joy He has in you, the helping hand He continually holds out to you! The understanding of our failures, His forgiveness and His desire to draw us closer and closer to Himself, until we become one with Him. Oh the joy of knowing we are so loved by The Father! To know His watch care and closeness through our whole life and on through eternity! *Thank You, Thank You, Thank You, Father!*

Laura Galvin

ONE STEP AT A TIME

Father, how do we get to where we're going?
One step at a time child, with your hand in mine
Father, how do I get from where I am,
to where you want me to be?
Look into My face child, and you will see the answers
Then you will realize that you can
only take these steps with Me
A prayer here and one there, the same with right choices
Before you know it, child, we'll end up where we're going!

Morning by morning he wakens me
and opens my understanding to his will
Isaiah 50:4b, TLB

COMES THE WHISPER

WHAT I WHISPER
IN YOUR EARS
PROCLAIM FROM THE
HOUSETOPS!
MATTHEW 10:27B TLB

WHISPERS

SIT ON MY LAP

Sit here on my lap, child, while I tell you a story

When my Son was young
I sent Him to the world to help them and save them
He was full of love, never did an unkind thing or hurt a soul
But they hated Him, spit on Him and killed Him!

How do you think my heart felt?
How do you think Mary's heart hurt?
The grief was unbearable!
How do you think I felt
When I had to turn my face away from Him for you?

I love you so much, child
That I was willing to do this and bear this pain for you
Please go tell my people this!
Tell them that I loved them enough to let my beloved Son
Be beaten and tortured for them
Tell them that I loved them enough to bear that grief for them
And allowed Him also to suffer and bear the grief for them
Tell them, child, tell them for Me!

For God so loved the world, that he gave his only begotten Son,
that whosoever believeth in him should not perish,
but have everlasting life.
John 3:16 KJV

WAITING FOR YOUR WHISPER

Father as I sit here by Your feet, resting in your presence
Content to be still, to be Yours and Yours alone
Knowing that into my silence, You will pour Your love
Your peace, Your joy, knowing no bounds

As I sit here in Your silence
Letting You be my God, my Everything
In this silence I wait for You
To whisper Your visions, Your plans

I wait for Your Power to transform me
I wait to mount up on eagle's wings
Your strength moving in me
And flowing out to others through me

Thank you, Father, for your stillness

Be still and know that I am God:
Psalms 46:10

WHAT ARE YOU OFFERING, FATHER?

The world is full of multitudes of people
Just wanting to be loved
Wanting to be peaceful
Not asking for much
What do You have to offer them, Father?
Can You explain it simply?

I have life to offer them, child
Hope above all hope
A firm foundation on which to stand
My Sons Precious Blood, was shed for them
Love unlike anything they've ever experienced
But most off all I offer MYSELF
To be their GOD, their FATHER, their EVERYTHING
But there is a high price to pay
Life for life, I gave My Son's life
What I'm asking is their life in return!
All their heart, all their soul, all their mind
I want to fill them with Myself
To pour Myself out on others through them
This is what I'm offering them, child
Would you please tell them for Me?

He tells us everything over and over again,
a line at a time and in such simple words!
Isaiah 28:10 TLB

And you must love the LORD your God
with all your heart, all your soul, and all your strength.
Deuteronomy 6:5 NL

RUN INTO MY PRESENSE

Remember, child, I see beyond your broken places
I and only I know the longing in your heart
I know your deep desire to do only what is good, right and true
I understand the longing in your heart to rewrite the past
This we cannot do, but child, just give the past to me
It's the only way you can ever be free, free to move forward
Free from the past, free to change, free to have a future

Don't try to hide your failure from Me
Like you would an earthly Father
You must know and understand that I love you
I love you so much that I sent my only Son to die for you
So that you could come right up to Me and climb on My lap
Please don't ever try to hide anything from Me
Run into My presence; let Me heal your hurts and scars

Child, there is nowhere else to go for healing!
Nowhere else to go to receive the love I'm offering you
I'm always here waiting for you to come to Me and be healed
I don't care what you've done or are doing, just come, run!
Don't be afraid or discouraged. I'm your Father
Just crawl on my lap and tell me all the things you long for Me to heal
I've been waiting so long for you, child
Jesus' precious blood is here to cover it all, past, present, future
Come, child, run, I love you more than you can ever know!

Come, let's talk this over! Says the Lord; no matter how deep the
stain of your sins, I can take it out and make you as clean as freshly
fallen snow. Even if you are stained as red as crimson,
I can make you white as wool!
Isaiah 1:18 TLB

God will keep his covenant of love with you . . .
He will love you and bless you.
Deuteronomy 7:12, 13 NIV

WHO AM I?

Write the words, You say, write how you feel
Write so that those who come behind may find the way
I hate writing when I'm not trusting
You or when I'm feeling fear
It makes me feel so lowly
Where's the super-Christian?
But super-Christian I'm not!
I'm just someone trying to draw near to You
Someone who loves You and is much loved by You
Someone who sometimes wanders off Your path
Goes astray in my mind, forgets what You've taught me
I feel such fear and anger and shame when I fall short,
Such disappointment, such unworthiness
Who am I? What is lying just ahead?
Will I be able to stand firm or will I fall flat on my face?
Who am I, Lord, that You should use me in Your army?
I who can be so afraid, who am I, Lord?

"This is what the LORD, the God of Israel, says: 'Write in a book
all the words I have spoken to you.'"
Jeremiah 30:2 NIV

He won't let you stumble, your Guardian God won't fall asleep.
Psalms 121:3 The Message

GOD puts the fallen on their feet again.
Psalms 147:6 The Message

You won't have to lift a hand in this battle; just stand firm, and
watch GOD's saving work for you take shape. Don't be afraid,
don't waver. March out boldly tomorrow--GOD is with you.
2 Chronicles 20:17 The Message

MUCH LOVED

You are a much loved child of the King
You are watched over by the Bright and Morning Star
You are loved beyond your belief
You are surrounded and held up by God Himself
You are precious to Me and honored and I love you
You are in training, child
If I don't allow you to have these feelings
How would you ever be able to help others?

Step out in faith, child, reach out and take My hand
Just stand and take one step, then we'll learn to take two
It's okay, child, I have you very carefully
under My watchful care

My response is to get down on my knees before the Father, this
magnificent Father who parcels out all heaven and earth. I ask him to
strengthen you by his Spirit--not a brute strength but a glorious inner
strength--that Christ will live in you as you open the door and invite
him in. And I ask him that with both feet planted firmly on love, you'll
be able to take in with all Christians the extravagant dimensions of
Christ's love. Reach out and experience the breadth! Test its length!
Plumb the depths! Rise to the heights! Live full lives, full in the
fullness of God. God can do anything, you know--far more than you
could ever imagine or guess or request in your wildest dreams! He
does it not by pushing us around but by working within us,
his Spirit deeply and gently within us.
Ephesians 3:14-20 The Message

STARTING OVER

Father, I'm not who I think I am
And not who you want me to be
But laying all that aside
Let's start with me giving You
My permission to fill me
To mold me, to make me
Who you want me to be
A person filled and consumed with You

May you experience the love of Christ,
though it is so great you will never fully understand it.
Then you will be filled with the fullness of it
and power that comes from God.
Ephesians 3:19 NLT

OLD THINGS
WILL FALL AWAY

Child, off the cross, off the throne
Into the center of your being
This is where I'll dwell
From now through eternity
Not only will I be in you
But I'll be over you

You will dwell in the shadow of My wings
Under My huge outstretched arms
You are Mine and Mine completely!
The old things will fall away
Without so much as a by your leave
They will be gone

You will look for them in vain
Instead you will find Me!
You will be consumed by Me!
This is your desire, isn't it, child?
You may have the desire of your heart
Since your desire is to delight in Me

Beware of the evil one; he would destroy you
But that shall not be so!
For I've chosen you to lead a mighty army for Me

My arms are around you, My heart will be in you
My heart will pour out through you, like a mighty river
My power will flow through you
You will never be the same!

Delight yourself also in the Lord and He will give you the
desires and secret petitions of your heart.
Psalms 37:4 TAB

WALKING ON GOD'S PROMISES

Father, as we walk this path of life
Help me to claim each promise in Your Word
As the sole of my foot steps upon these promises
Help me to make them mine, teach me
To use Your Word, to learn to trust in You
Word upon word, line upon line, promise upon promise
Thank You that as I walk Your path

Holding Your hand, eyes upon Your face
That You will teach me new and wonderful things
Day upon day, moment upon moment, year upon year
Truth upon truth, commandment upon commandment
That You will teach me how to love You
How to walk in all Your ways, how to hold fast to You
That You will drive out my enemies
That all this will be done, because of Your great love for me
Thank You Father for taking the time to walk with me

Therefore you shall lay these My words in your [mind and]
in your [entire] being... Deuteronomy 11:18

Every place upon which the sole of your foot shall tread
shall be yours... Deuteronomy 11:24A NAS

The steps of a [good] man are directed and established
of the Lord, when He delights in his way
[and He busies Himself with his every step].
Psalms 37:23 TAB

AND THE TWO BECAME ONE

Father, the song says
There's a place
Where when You breathe
We move

What a wonderful place
That must be
Will I ever be there
Father?

Will I ever be
That in tune with You?
That consumed?
That obedient?
Will I, Father?

Child, it's so simple
Put your hand in Mine
Look into My face
Walk with Me
Talk with Me
Laugh with Me
And the two of us
Will become one

Put your hand in Mine
Let's walk together

It's God's Spirit in a person,
the breath of the Almighty One,
that makes wise insight possible.
Job 32:18 The Message

GOD IS KIND, BUT
HE'S NOT SOFT.
IN KINDNESS HE TAKES US
FIRMLY BY THE HAND
AND LEADS US INTO A
RADICAL LIFE-CHANGE.
ROMANS 2:4B THE MESSAGE

CHANGES COMING

CHANGES COMING

I'm confused, Father, there are so many changes
Changes in my life, changes in my friends' lives
Changes in the church, changes in everything
What does it all mean?

Child, there are many changes ahead
You must prepare your heart for what is coming
The Wind of My Holy Spirit is blowing across the land
Touching the high places, touching the low places
Touching the hearts of My people and My people to come

My eyes are searching, My heart is longing
For people who want to serve Me with all their heart
For people who want to change and be moved by My Spirit
People who will be warriors and fight the battle for Me
With My power, My blood, My name

My eyes are searching, My Spirit is empowering
Stranger things than you've ever seen are ahead
Take My hand, child, come along with Me

These are things you won't want to miss
Please don't be left behind in a changeless world
Please don't miss the Wind of My Spirit
As it blows across the land, looking for people to be used
Come, child, take My hand, you don't want to miss this!

For the eyes of the Lord search the whole earth in order to
strengthen those whose hearts are fully committed to him.
2 Chronicles 16:9 NLT

LIFT US, FATHER, SO WE CAN SEE

Oh Father, You are a Great and Mighty God
Lord of the heavens and earth, Lord of the sea
Oh, Father, lift me high and hold me up so I can see
I want to see things like You see them, through Your eyes
Eyes of Love, Love that comes from Your heart
I want to see Your Truth, so it can set me free

Father, raise up Your believers into an army
An army carrying the banner of Your truths
Endowed with Your Power that comes from above
Because You are the truth that sets men free

Oh Father, open our eyes and let us see
Teach us how to have victory
As we carry Your Word to the lost and bound
It is Your truth that binds the enemy
And sets Your people free

Father, help us to understand, that in us, is Your greatness
We want to sing Your battle cry, Victory, Victory!
Freedom to the bound, life to the dying, love to the unloved!
Oh Father, lift us high
Hold us in Your arms so we can see

The precepts of the Lord are right, rejoicing the heart;
the commandments of the Lord is pure and
bright, enlightening the eyes. Palms19:8 TAB

THE FEAR OF CHANGE

Why do we fear change so much?
Stepping into the unknown
Trying to hang on to the past
Fearing the future
How do we change, Father?

Remember, child
I am always with you
Seek My direction
Search for My path
But always, look into My face

I can walk you through anything
And bless you greatly
If you'll only allow Me to
My peace is brought by faith
Faith in Me, not faith in your venture

Just trust Me, child
To work out your circumstances
No matter what they are
You can trust Me!
Will you, child?
Don't be afraid!

Just jump into My arms!
They are wide open and ready to catch you!

Jesus shouted to the crowds, "if you trust me,
you are really trusting God who sent me"
Matthew 12:44 NLT

PLEASE, FATHER

I WANT TO OBEY!!!!!!!!!
Please, help me obey, please, please!
I just want to do things Your way, please!
Please, please, Father, please help me!
I need Your desire to be obedient
Your power to carry through
Your love to forgive myself
When I fail

But, most of all
I just want more of You!!
Please, help me, Father
To do Your will
Please, bless me with the desire to obey
And Your will to carry through
Please, Father, please!
Thank You Father before I see!

Keep me far from every wrong; help me, undeserving
as I am, to obey your laws, for I have chosen to do right.
I cling to your commands and follow them as closely as I can.
Lord, don't let me make a mess of things. If you will only
help me to want your will, then I will follow your laws
even more closely. Psalms 119:29-32 TLB

THE CONTROLLER

Why do I need to control everything, Lord? Why?
Why can't I let you do the controlling?
Why do I have the need to herd and control
my little flock of family?
When really it's You who are our Shepherd!
If only they would do things your way, Lord!
If only *I* would do things your way, Lord!
If only they would make the right choices, Lord
If only *I* would make the right choices, Lord!

I can see so clearly the right choices for them
Much easier than I can see the right choices for myself
If they could only choose You above all others, they would win!
If I could choose You above all others, I would win!
I can't seem to control myself Lord, but I will try to help them!

When I couldn't control the situations around me
I controlled myself to survive and not think about them
I couldn't control my bad habits, so I made excuses for them and
blamed others
I couldn't control my family, so I controlled myself not to be hurt
I couldn't control God, so I tried to control
what people thought of Him!
I needed to stay in control, I thought
So we wouldn't ruin our lives and the lives of those around us!
If only I could have stayed in control, but I just couldn't
I'm sorry, Lord, I tried so hard to control--for You, I thought
But the job is just too big for me
I couldn't make any of us change!

He'll complete in detail what he's decided about me,
and whatever else he determines to do.
Job 23:14 The Message

20

THE CONTROLLED

We all came, we all went
We made mistakes and hurt and grieved
Ourselves and each other
All of my controlling was for naught, nothing changed!
No one would do what I said!
And I couldn't do what You said!!
Around and around we went, year after year
For forever, it seemed

So I found that the controllers don't really control
We really only spin our wheels!
We feel such disappointment and delusion
When the chess pieces won't move!
We feel such agony when we don't change
What else can I say? What else can I do to make them move?

I know the answer! I know what I can do!
Dear Heavenly Father
I can enter your rest and peace at last!
I can turn the controlling over to you!

Please Father, start with me, be my controller!

I love you, child

I love You, Father

So he will do for me all he has planned.
He controls my [*our*] destiny.
Job 23:14 NLT

FREEDOM OR STUBBORNNESS?

When I wouldn't make You Lord of my life
I traded Your freedom
For my stubbornness
The enemy blinded my eyes
And told me I won
I would control my life
I would make my decisions
I would do my best
Because, surely I knew what was best for me
I had a plan, a vision
I knew you put me here to do my best
And in my heart I knew
You really didn't want to be bothered with
Such a small thing as me
When someone told me that was untrue!
That You wanted to run my life
And You could do it so much better than I could
I balked in fear
To lose control was an unbearable thought!
So what will I do?
Will I trade my stubbornness
For Your freedom and control?
Will I choose to grow in You?
Or will I remain the same
In bondage to what I want to think is true?

My counsel for you is simple and straightforward: Just go ahead with what you've been given. You received Christ Jesus, the Master; now live him. You're deeply rooted in him. You're well constructed upon him. You know your way around the faith. Now do what you've been taught. School's out; quit studying the subject and start living it! *And let your living spill over into thanksgiving.*
Colossians 2:6-7 The Message
I will walk in freedom, for I have devoted myself to your commandments.
Psalms 119:45 NLT

DIVINE POWER

Oh Father, *thank You* that You're right beside me
When I am quailing in fear, wincing from uncertainty
Thank You for Your patience as You move me along
Towards what You have always had in mind for me

Please forgive me for my stubbornness
For the strongholds in me, some set in place by choice
Some there from things beyond my control

Thank You that many are gone and mostly forgotten
Thank You that You're close to me, holding me, teaching me
As we embark on getting rid of the remaining ones

Thank You that You've made my mind sharp and clear
Full of Your Word and Your instructions for me

For though we live in the world,
we do not wage war as the world does.
The weapons we fight with are not the weapons of the world.
On the contrary, they have divine power to demolish strongholds
2 Corinthians 10:3-4 NIV

MAKING ME BRAND NEW

Why can't I be who I want to be?
Why can't I change faster?

But, *thank You* that You are changing me
Little by little day by day
With the turning of a thought here
A choice there, a whisper of encouragement
Line upon line, word upon word
Changing on the inside
Where no one can see

But You're changing me for good
Changing me for keeps
Changing my heart and thoughts
Changing the center of my being
Bubbling Your life and truth in me
Letting it wash through me
Cleansing me, making me brand new
Healing hurts, breaking bondage's
Setting me free, to be who You need me to be
Thank you, Father, for changing me

Now your thoughts and attitudes must be
constantly changing for the better. Yes, you
must be a new and different person, holy and
good. Clothe yourself with this new nature.
Ephesians 4:23-24 TLB

CHILD, I DELIGHT IN YOU

Father, I love You more than words can say
How I love to hear You say, Child, I love you
There are no sweeter words to my ears
My spirit rejoices as I hear you sing over me
Child, I love you so, you are so dear to me

Father, I love you so much, take my heart
Draw me ever closer so that we become one
Consume me, so that my thoughts are Your thoughts
I give my heart to the wind of Your Holy Spirit
Refresh me, set me on fire with a new and deeper love
A love for You that passes all human understanding
I want more of You, Father, fill me fuller
Please use me to bubble over on Your children

Child, I delight in you, I am filling you with Myself
I sing over you, because I love you, you are Mine
I am your God, I will walk with you throughout eternity
I will give you a love for Me that surpasses human
understanding
I will make you mine, inside and out, you are My creation
Thank you for allowing Me to mold and form you as I planned
You are special to Me and I love you dearly!

The Lord your God is with you, he is mighty to save.
He will take great delight in you, he will quiet you with his love,
he will rejoice over you with singing
Zephaniah 3:17 NIV

LOOKING FORWARD TO CHANGE

Father, I see I'm starting to look forward to changes
I'm seeing things differently, through eyes that come from You
Things that seemed impossible are looking easier
I find myself looking forward to doing them
Instead of cringing in fear

You're giving me new eyes to see
You're showing me that I am more than a conqueror in You
You're teaching me to look the enemy in the face
Bind him, and move on, not looking to the left or right
Keeping my eyes on You, marching straight towards my destiny
Of helping people walk in Your freedom

To arrive there, I must myself be free
Thank You for freeing me, step by step, day by day
Thank You, Father, I love You so much
I reach out my hand, I feel Your touch
I feel Your love, Your power, Your grace flow through me
I feel Your kiss on my face as I move along in Your plan for me

You are my destiny, my joy, my love, my life
Thank you, Father, for freeing me, step by step, day by day

You're welcome, child
This was my plan from the beginning for you

So let's keep focused on that goal, those of us who want everything
God has for us. If any of you have something else in mind,
something less than total commitment, God will clear your
blurred vision--you'll see it yet! Now that we're on the right
track, let's stay on it.
Philippians 3:14 The Message

BURSTING INTO FREEDOM

Father, I'm ready to burst forth into freedom
Like a sunbeam hiding behind a cloud
To burst forth into Your greatness and grandeur
Into freedom that comes only from You

I stand perched on the threshold of this adventure
Awaiting the realization of this dream and desire
I just need a small push from You, Father
To get from where I am to where I want to be

Then I need for You to run with me daily
To carry me and encourage me, to hold me when I'm tired
And to give me a nudge when I want to hide behind
the cloud again

Child, I love you, I will run this race with you
I will carry you when you're tired, I will nudge you along
I will love you and give you the desires of your heart
You will walk in freedom through your life adventure
Let's go, it's time to burst forth like a sunbeam!

Freedom is what we have--Christ has set us free! Stand,
then, as free men, and do not allow yourselves to become slaves
again. Galatians 5:11 Today's English Version

THE FREEDOM SONG

I sit here
Watching, listening, participating
Speaking the healing to come forth

Wonder of wonders, praise of praises
Glory to the Father, Glory to the Son
Glory to the Spirit, the precious Three in One!

I watch as You restore souls
Bring life into bones, and cleanse cells
Minds are washed clean
The power of fear is loosed, and must fall away!

We arise in Your freedom!
Freedom, freedom, freedom
Freedom to the bound, to Your children
To the hurt and wounded

Step by step by step, freedom
Healing, in Jesus name!
Blessed are we to be the chosen ones

As the Dove flies
The Lord rejoices
And the Father God sings
Freedom, freedom, freedom!

The Spirit of the Sovereign LORD is on me, because the LORD
has anointed me to preach good news to the poor. He has sent me to
bind up the brokenhearted, to proclaim freedom for the captives and
release from darkness for the prisoners. . .
Isaiah 61:1 NIV

He Will Make The Darkness
Bright Before Them And Smooth And
Strighten Out The Road Ahead.
Isaiah 42:16b TLB

THE PATH

YOU POINTED THE WAY

Dear Lord Jesus
I walked with you so long
Side by side, my arm in Yours
Year after year after year
When you walked I walked
When you sat I sat
When you stood I stood
Then one day you brought
Me to my Father's feet
To a place where I met
The Blessed Holy Spirit
A Person yet unknown to me
Even though I'd heard of Him
You let go of my hand
And pointed out the Comforter to me
As He and I walked on I grieved
That Your presence seemed to be gone
You reminded me that it was the same
When you left Your disciples
The men who knew You so well
You told them You had to go
So that the Comforter could come
How confused they must have felt
Please teach me, Father
About all the parts of Yourself

I have told you these things while I am still with you. But the Comforter (Counselor, Helper, Intercessor, Advocate, Strengthener, Standby), the Holy Spirit, Whom the Father will send in My name [in My place, to represent Me and act on My behalf], He will teach you all things. And He will cause you to recall (will remind you of, bring to your remembrance) everything I have told you. Peace I leave with you; My [own] peace I now give and bequeath to you. Not as the world gives do I give to you. Do not let your hearts be troubled, neither let them be afraid. [Stop allowing yourselves to be agitated and disturbed; and do not permit yourselves to be fearful and intimidated and cowardly and unsettled.] John 14:25-27 TAB

THE PATH

Father, remember all the years Jesus walked with me?
We were always on that path walking toward You
Year after year, lesson after lesson, He taught me so many lessons
How to walk, how to wait, how to love, how to give
On and on, year after year. Finally there we were at Your throne
I remember we stayed there awhile and continued learning
Then one day we started down another path
It was a sharp turn to Your left, my right
Father, I've never really understood this
Would You please tell me about this so that I can understand?

I love you, child. When you came to My feet, it was a symbol
A symbol of freedom, a symbol that one part of the journey was done
But there is more, so much more, child
There is a walk with My Holy Spirit that never ends
There are longings in your heart that it will take eternity to fill

Look at My face, child, as you walk this path with the Holy Spirit
You must look into My face continually minute by
minute, day by day
This path doesn't take you away from Me, it draws you closer
I'm watching you every minute, I'm lovingly holding
you each step you take
Child, not everyone walks this path. Many are content
to stop at my feet
But, child, I looked into your heart and saw that you wanted more
More of Me, to love Me more, to walk closer with Me
I've honored that desire of your heart, child, because
you delight in me

Take My hand, child, you'll never believe what lies ahead
Don't worry; I walk this path with you day by day, minute by minute

I will instruct you and teach you in the way which you should go.
I will counsel you with My eye upon you. Psalms 32:8 NIV

WHEN TIME STANDS STILL

There comes a moment in time
When things change
Time stands still for a second
And your life makes a turn
Sometimes we see it clearly
But often we're completely unaware

An unkind word is spoken
We're hurt or broken
But we dry our eyes
And continue on, never quite realizing
That we made a turn
And the enemy gained a foothold

Other times "THE WORD" is spoken
We glimpse a truth
We choose to forgive and be forgiven
We've made a turn on the pathway to Heaven
A moment when time stood still
And we walk on in freedom and healing!

You have made known to me the path of life;
you will fill me with joy in your presence,
with eternal pleasures at your right hand.
Psalms 16:11

34

TRUST AND FAITH

Dear Father, what are trust and faith?
Where do I find them? Where do they hide?
One minute I think I have them, the next minute they're gone
I want to cry with frustration as I look for them again
Tell me, Father, where do they go?

Child, faith and trust are very strange things
When you look for them, you won't find them
It's only by looking at Me that you'll be able to see
So take My hand and look into My face
The amazing thing is, faith and trust will follow

Your Heavenly Father knows that you need them all.
Set your heart first on his kingdom and his goodness,
and all these things will come to you as a matter of course.
Matthew 6:32b-33 Phillips M E

WALKING IN OBEDIENCE

Obedience is my plan!
Take my hand, Lord, as I walk this path
Made easy because of our love for each other
Thank You that it can be fun
Hand in hand we wander down this path
Towards the Promised Land

Promises of a great future
Promises of better health
Promises of less pain
Promises of a greater closeness
Because of the joy in my heart
Over my complete obedience

Onward and upward to the Promised Land
Thanks, Father!

And this is love:
that we walk in obedience to his commands.
As you have heard from the beginning,
his command is that you walk in love.
2 John 1:6 NIV

WHY OBEDIENCE ?

Because I recognize Who You are
I fall to my knees in awe
Because You're my Lord and Master
My heart is filled with love
Because I know Your great love for me
My will chooses to obey Your every word
I do not do this to acquire Your love
I do it because I <u>have</u> Your love
Not so I can become Your child
But because I <u>am</u> Your child
Because I know there's no other way
That can fill me with Your peace and joy
You are my God; I am Your child
Please, Father
Be obedient through me

GOD, O God of Israel,
there is no God like you in the skies above or on the earth below,
who unswervingly keeps covenant with his servants
and unfailingly loves them
while they sincerely live in obedience to your way.
2 Chronicles 6:14 The Message

Your obedience will give you a long life
on the soil that GOD promised to give your ancestors and their
children, a land flowing with milk and honey.
Deuteronomy 11:9 The Message

THERE WOULD BE NO LIFE WITHOUT YOU

Father, I love You so much
Thank You for walking with me today
For helping me walk the walk
I've been asking You to

I don't want to lose You, Father
There would be no life without You
To have known You
And lost You would be incomprehensible!

There would be nothing but emptiness in my life
Void and darkness would be upon me
I cannot imagine the grief and loneliness
That would surround me
This is too terrible for me to even think on!

Thank You for making a way for me
For sending Your Son
For bringing Your never-ending light into my life
Thank You for giving me eternity with You

For Your love and kindness are better to me than life itself.
How I praise you! I will bless you as long as I live, lifting up
my hands to you in prayer. At last I shall be fully satisfied;
I will praise you with great joy. Psalms 63:3-5 TLB

THE WOMAN BY THE SIDE OF THE ROAD

An older woman stands along the road in the pouring rain
In one hand she holds a sign
In the other an umbrella
The sign she holds reads:
BABIES KILLED AT THIS HOTEL

I've passed her in this spot many times through the years
I honk the horn, I wave, to let her know I appreciate her
It comes over me like a wave, tears fill my eyes
Why is she so dedicated?
Why don't I have the urge to right this wrong?

"Child," my Father says, "This is the job I've given her
Not the one I've given you"

I drive on through the rain pondering this truth
God has given each of us gifts and jobs to do
Show me, Father
What is the job You have for me?

God's various gifts are handed out everywhere;
but they all originate in God's Spirit.
God's various ministries are carried out everywhere;
but they all originate in God's Spirit.
God's various expressions of power are in action everywhere;
but God himself is behind it all.
Each person is given something to do that shows who God is:
Everyone gets in on it, everyone benefits.
All kinds of things are handed out by the Spirit,
and to all kinds of people! The variety is wonderful.
I Corinthians 12:4 - 7 The Message

YOUR WAY

Please, Father God
Help me live my life Your way
Only Your way
Help me never to choose disobedience
You have given me many words
For my ears to hear
Many things for my eyes to see
Please be obedient through me
Set my feet on Your path
Take my hand
Lead me in the way of obedience
My eyes are upon You
And my trust is totally in You
I can only do this as You do it through me
Thank you, Father

God is kind, but he's not soft. In kindness he takes us
firmly by the hand and leads us into a radical life change.
Romans 2:4 The Message

THE WAY MAKER

Father, thank You that You're the Way Maker
What a neat thing to think about
As we come to this large crossroads in our life
As we start down a path that seems like the right way
That You Yourself take the time to stand in front of the path
With Your huge arms outstretched saying, "Not yet"
You're not quite ready for this turn, wait just awhile

Take My hand, child, look into My face
I have some things to show you first
Things that your eyes have seen and your ears have heard
But your heart has not understood as yet

When you walk this path, child, I want you to
have a hungry heart
To hunger and thirst after life-changing knowledge of Me
Do not fear. My arms are around you, My eyes are on you
You were born to serve me, that's why I gave you life

Take my hand, child, look into My face, My way is the best
I have things for you that are above and beyond
Your wildest imagination!

You're blessed when you've worked up a good appetite for God.
He's food and drink in the best meal you'll ever eat.
Matthew 5:6 The Message

HE COUNTS MY EVERY STEP

Father, thank You that You love me
You see my ways and count my every step
Your arms are around me
Your hand holds mine
If I fall, You gently pick me up
You dry my tears and brush me off
You explain the plan to me once more
Then You gently set my feet on Your path again

Does He not see my ways and count my every step?
Job 31:4 NIV

THE RED SEA

Father, I see the Red Sea looming up ahead of me
It looks so huge and overpowering, it looks like I'll be trapped!
It even looks like I might drown; I need to look away
So here I go, I take my eyes off the problem
And I put them on You

Now what do I see?

I see my Father, my Master, my Lord, my King
I see my Provider, who has promised me everything
I see the One who made me, the One who holds my hand
The One who led me down His path since childhood
I see the One who loves me, as if there were only me
I see the Great I Am--the Beginning and the End
I see You, Father, the One who chose my path before I was born

So when I see satan waving flags, screaming, Red Sea! Red Sea!
I'll just turn and look into Your face of love
I'll hear You say, Take My hand, child
You'll be amazed at the way I open that Red Sea
Remember I've come to give You life and
give it to you abundantly

I love You, Father

I love you, child!

By faith they passed through the Red Sea as
though they were passing through dry land.
Hebrews 11:29 NAS

WALKING IN GOD'S REST

Father, I want to walk in Your rest
What does this mean? How do we walk in Your rest?

It means, child, that you come to Me in the morning
That you stay with Me in your thoughts throughout the day
That you whisper you love Me, as I whisper I love you
That you *give Me thanks continually* in all things
That you strive <u>gently</u> to see My face and know My will

This is what it means to walk in My rest
Come, child, take My hand, let's walk in it together
You'll love it!

Are you tired? Worn out? Burned out on religion?
Come to me. Get away with me and you'll recover your life.
I'll show you how to take a real rest.
Walk with me and work with me--watch how I do it.
Learn the unforced rhythms of grace.
I won't lay anything heavy or ill-fitting on you.
Keep company with me and you'll learn to live freely and lightly.
Matthew 11:28-30 The Message

YOUR CHILD I AM

Father, talk to my heart
Cry out to my ears
Bring Your song on the Spirit Wind
Your child I am

Give me love that I can see
Give me thoughts above the now
Father, my heart cries out to You
To see and understand as You do

To see the path to run the race
To reach up and touch Your face
These are my desires, Father
Are they Yours, too?

Of course they are, child

The Lord is fair in everything he does, and
full of kindness. He is close to all who call on him
sincerely. He fulfills the desires of those who reverence
and trust him. . . Psalms 145:17-18A TLB

WHAT IS MY DESTINY?

Father, I came to you awhile back
"What is my destiny?" I cried
I can't see past the end of the day
And often that's a struggle
If You have a destiny for me, Father
Then You must show me because I can't see it!

So I turned my face toward Yours
And went about my daily life
Trying to spend time with You
Trying to seek Your face, trying to put You first
Finding my joy in You, making You my life
Step by step, day by day, hour by hour

As I followed after Your Holy Spirit
I found myself doing new things
Things that I never thought I would do
Or that I didn't know how to do
I began to see You molding and shaping me
Turning me in new directions
Gently showing me that in Your strength
I can become all that You meant for me to be

But those who follow after the Holy Spirit find themselves
doing those things that please God.
Following after the Holy Spirit leads to life and peace.
Romans 8:5b-6a TLB

YOU HOLD THE FUTURE

Father
You hold the future
In the palm of Your hand
It is Your gift to us
A surprise package
I'm sure
If we only knew
If we could only see
What would we think?
What would we choose?
To change right now
How would we face it?
Would we laugh?
Would we cry?

Father
You hold our hands
Please keep our feet
On Your path
And our eyes on Your face
That's all we need to know
As we run this race
That You love us!
And that we walk in Your Grace!

I want you to go out there and walk - better yet run! - on the road
God called you to travel. I don't want any of you sitting around
on your hands. I don't want anyone strolling off, down some path
that goes nowhere. And mark that you do this with humility and
discipline - not in fits and starts, but steadily, pouring yourselves out
for each other in acts of love, alert at noticing differences and quick
at mending fences.
Ephesians 4:1b-3 The Message

DON'T LOOK BACK, CHILD

Don't look back, child, the path you've come is long
Look only into My face
I'm making the way straight

Don't look back at past failures
Over the long winding road
Back over things you wish you could change

Don't look back, child, just take My hand
The path is onward and upward
From now throughout eternity we'll walk together

Don't look back, child, it gives the devil a foothold
Just leave the past behind
Walk on towards the future
The good things walk with you
The bad are left behind

Put your eyes upon My face, your hand in Mine
Come on, child, I'll help you climb

He will make the darkness bright before them and smooth
and straighten out the road ahead.
Isaiah 42:16b TLB

HIGHER GROUND, IS OUR CRY

Please, Father, take us to higher ground
We want to step out in faith
Catching Your hand, slipping our arm in Yours
Walking with You, full of love and joy
As we make our way to higher ground

Father, we're tired of crawling and struggling
in our upward way
We're ready to move out in faith
Marching to the mighty call of the Savior
Eyes upon Your face, Father
Led by Your blessed Spirit
Higher ground! higher ground! is our cry!
Till we stand before Your throne and with You become One

Move us up to higher ground, Father, lead the way
Higher ground, clear in our view, Your face we see clearly
As we leave behind the things that were dragging us down

Higher ground! higher ground! This is our cry!
***Thank You, Father,* for teaching us how to walk in victory!**

I hear your heart's cry, child
Follow Me, I'll lead the way up Victory Hill
Your burdens will drop, your tears will fall
As we walk this life-changing way
Take my hand, child, you'll never be the same

God be praised, he gives us the victory through
our Lord Jesus Christ
1 Corinthians 15:57 New English Bible

Nothing In All Creation Can Hide From Him. Everything Is Naked And Exposed Before His Eyes.this Is The God To Whom We Must Explain All That We Have Done.

Hebrews 4:13 NLT

NAKED BEFORE THE THRONE

THE CARES OF THIS WORLD

Father God, Lord Jesus, Blessed Holy Spirit
I'm here to set aside the cares of this world
I want to fall in love with You, more than I ever have before
That is the desire of my heart, so what's hindering me?

Selfishness, lust for things of this world
Desire not to face obedience and discipline
Forgive me, Father, I see myself not facing truth
So, out of fear and need not to look things as they are
I fill my life with other good things
But down underneath I know I'm escaping the truth

You've called and called, "Come away, my beloved"
But for some reason I was too tired (or busy) to make it
On and on it went until I stopped hearing You call

I've asked you to show me the things in me that don't please You
I'm beginning to see--and it makes me so sad

satan steps in with his pounding condemnation:
What you thought you were was all a lie, garbage!
Look at what you're really like, yuk! And everybody else can see
What will you do?
There's too much garbage for you to ever change!

NAKED BEFORE THE THRONE

Boy, did he hit the nail on the head!
Too much for me to ever change
Now what do I do? Things really look bleak
I know, I'll turn my eyes to my Father's face
He will take care of it--<u>I will seek Him first!</u>
Then all these, glaring faults will fall away
I will fall in love with Him, more and more,
Until I will be like Him
Keep calling, Father, please keep calling me

I waited patiently for God to help me;
then he listened and heard my cry.
He lifted me out of the pit of despair,
out from the bog and the mire,
and set my feet on a hard, firm path
and steadied me as I walked along.
He has given me a new song to sing,
of praises to our God.
Psalms 40:1-3 TLB

CONDEMNATION

CONDEMNATION! What is it?
It's terrible! It's rotten!
It comes straight from the pit of hell!
It comes to twist and torture you!
To harm you and to hurt you!
To lie to you and torment you!

It tells you you're wrong and stupid!
You've made wrong decisions!
There's no one worse than you!
You're a loser and you'll never win!

It screams in your face!
It hits you in your middle!
It strips you of your peace!
It fills you with fear and sickness!

It laughs, you'll never be different!
You really blew it this time!
It leads you into despair and hopelessness!
It's black, it's evil, it's satan's way!

But most of all, it's a LIE!!
That comes straight from the pit of hell!!
RECOGNIZE THE ENEMY, CHILD!!!

For God sent not his Son into the world to condemn the world;
but that the world through him might be saved.
John 3:17 KJV

CONVICTION FROM ABOVE

Now, child, let Me tell you about conviction
It's different from condemnation
No harshness, no accusations, no torment
It never screams in your face
Conviction is gentle, leading you, not accusing you
It draws you in the right direction
If you're headed another way
It lets you know you're not pleasing Me
That you're grieving Me
But it does so very gently and calmly and steadily
My conviction says, "No child, this isn't My will for you
You will be harmed, walk this way, follow Me"
It says, "Child, I want you to stop and turn your face to Me"
Sometimes I force you gently by laying down the alternative
I do this because I can see your future
And I know what's best for you
At the moment this is the last thing you can see
Because your eyes are blinded by desire for what you want now
I call you and draw you away from that
So you will keep to My path
You can be sure of one thing when I say, "Don't do that!"
It is for your own good
And against My perfect will for your life
When you feel uncomfortable and agitated
It's not coming from Me
It is caused by your unwillingness to walk My way
Be thankful for that uncomfortable feeling, child
When it's gone, you have hardened your heart to My call
Then the way back is harder and longer
But child, there's always a way back
Today, hear Me calling
Come back, child, I love you so much

Today when you hear him calling,
do not harden your heart against him. Hebrews 4:7 TLB

HIDDEN THINGS

Are you ready to stand before the Father naked?
Naked on the outside, completely open on the inside?
No hidden doors, nothing covered by anything?

Only when you are ready to do this
Can you then be totally healed and set free
Free of bondage's, free of secrets, free of the hidden things
Free to be clean, free to be healed, free to be free

Can you begin to understand His love for you is so great
That He doesn't hold these hidden things against you
He doesn't love you any less

He loves you so much that
His heart cries when He sees you carefully hiding things
That are trying to kill you and destroy you
Child, he calls, "Come to Me, come to Me so you can be free"

No creature has any cover from the sight of God; everything lies
naked and exposed before the eyes of him with whom we have to
deal. Seeing that we have a great High Priest who has passed through
the heavens, Jesus the Son of God, let us hold firmly to our faith. For
ours is no High Priest who cannot sympathize with our weaknesses-
-he himself has shared fully in all our experiences of temptation,
except that he never sinned. Let us therefore approach the throne
of grace with fullest confidence, that we may receive mercy for our
failures and grace to help in the hour of need.
Hebrews 4:13-16 Phillips Modern English

NAKED BEFORE GOD AND MAN

Well, Father, here I stand, naked before You and man
I hate it, I hate the hurt and raw pain of the past!
And the fear of the future, write the words, You say
Make them plain, who am I? I cry!
Why do we have to dig up the hidden things
Hurts and shame, things I've so carefully smoothed over
Things I've covered and thought I'd forgotten?
Why do they have to come up now? Why do I have to be naked?
Why must my protections be stripped away? Why, Father, why?
What good can it possibly do?
Child, can you please trust Me? Can you look into My face?
The pain you feel now is so small compared to the good to come
I want you to be free to walk with Me, free from the past
Free from the burdens you carry. I want you to understand
That without Me you will always be naked and ashamed
It is only by walking close to Me that you'll ever be free
Can you please *give Me thanks* and trust Me?
You must trust Me with your past, your present and your future
Who else loves you as I do? Who else can you trust but Me?
Take My hand, child, look into My face
I am giving you what You asked of Me, a way to be free
A way to help those who come behind you
A way to get rid of the things that are grieving Me
The things you weren't aware were dragging you down
Remember, child, I am here to help you and free you
Please let Me

The Lord God, compassionate and gracious,
slow to anger, and abounding in loving kindness and truth;
who keeps loving-kindness for thousands, who forgives iniquity,
transgression and sin.
Exodus 34:6b-7a NAS

NAKED

Child, when you walk with the Master
You are clothed in beautiful crimson
That is how others will see you
That is how I will see you

It is satan who will try to convince you
Of your nakedness and faults
It is not how We see you
We see you with the SON streaming over you
Standing in a Holy Valley
Standing before the Throne
We see you as reaching out
And touching the lives of others

Wake up, child! Come out of your slumber!
Recognize the enemy and what he's trying to do to you
Stand up! Shout the Victory!
You are a child of the King!
Covered by His Crimson Blood!
Bow down to no one but the Master!
You are not naked!
You are clothed in My righteousness!

Wake up! take up your weapons!
And prepare to win the Battle!
With My Name! My Word! My Blood!

I love you, child!!!

But now you belong to Christ Jesus, and though you once
were far away from God, now you have been brought very near to him
because of what Jesus Christ has done for you with his blood.
Ephesians 2:13 TLB

DIAMOND DAYS

**Child let me change your hard doubting days
Into diamond days**

**Let me give you the power to
Climb out of the darkest hour**

**Let Me dig beyond your hidden things
Let me set you free**

Please, child

***Thank You, Father,* before I see**

He reveals deep and hidden things;
he knows what lies in darkness,
and light dwells with him.
Daniel 2:22 NIV

CHILD, IT'S ONLY WHAT I CAN DO

Child, there is nothing you can do
There's only what I can do

Father, I sit along side Your feet
Bound to You with strong cords of love
Stillness pervades my spirit
And is entering my soul
I feel Your hand on my head
I am at peace

You have said
This is where the weary come to rest
Weary from the pursuit of freedom
From chasing change and obedience
Weary at failing
So I come to you in silence

Waiting instead upon Your timing
Your peace and joy
Your freedom, Your power
Waiting for You to do something or nothing
What ever pleases you, Master

But those who wait for the Lord [who expect, look for, and hope in Him] shall change and renew their strength and power; as eagles [mount up to the sun]; they shall run and not be weary, they shall walk and not faint or become tired.
Isaiah 40:31 TAB

ASK FOR GOD'S POWER

Child, come bow down before Me
The time has come for Me to anoint you
From this time forth My power will flow through you
As you touch others, it will be Me touching them
As you pray for the sick, it will be Me Who heals them
As you fight the demons, it will be Me fighting them
As you bind the spirits, it will be with My power
As you loose My Spirit, it will be Me flowing into them!

How I love you, child, I love you so much
You have not, because you ask not!
There are so many things to be done
Ask! Set Me free to move on behalf of your people
Your town, your world, your life
My power abides in you, child, use it!

Now glory be to God who by his mighty
power at work within us is able to do far
more than we would ever dare to ask or even
dream of--infinitely beyond our highest
prayers, desires, thoughts, or hopes
Ephesians 3:20 TLB

AGAIN?

My child, though you walk through the rivers I will be with you
I will comfort you and love you
My peace will pass over you like a light dusting
It will cover you and cling to you, it will shine upon you
When you feel alone and unworthy, look into My face
That is when I show up the best and most
I love you!
Do not look at where you've been
Do not look at where you are now
Look only at Me and where you're going
So many times you've failed; it means nothing
Turn your eyes to Me, look to the victory
You can never, and have never, been able to do it on your own
I love you, I'm rooting for you, you need no other
Let's walk down this path once again
This time it'll be different, this time it'll be true
Come, child, take My hand and let me walk with you
Don't look at the past, don't look at the failures
Look into my face, I'll make all things new
Come, child, look into My face and take My hand
I'll show you things you never thought you could do
I love you, child
Thank You, Father! Here's my hand and heart
My mind and spirit
Turn my eyes to Your face

For I know the plans I have for you, says the Lord.
They are plans for good
and not for evil, to give you a future and a hope. In those days when
you pray I will listen. You will find me when you seek me, if you
look for me in earnest.
Jeremiah 29:11-13 TLB

ANOTHER CHANCE

In the morning stillness
I feel my heart
Beating to your tune
I feel my blood coursing
As the Holy Spirit
Surges through me
I feel my hand reaching for You
Welcoming another day
Another chance to do things
Your way

Another day
Another chance
Another day
Another chance
Thank you
Father

And I am convinced and sure of this very thing,
that He who began a good work in you will continue
until the day of Jesus Christ [right up to the time of His return],
developing [that good work] and perfecting and bringing it to full
completion in you.
Philippians 1:6 TAB

FATHER, PLEASE HEAL YOUR BROKEN PEOPLE

Father, help us to understand that you are able to repair us
Help us to open our hearts and expose our hurts and brokenness
Show us the roots of our anguish, so we can be free
Pour Your oil of healing over our wounds

Let us not argue with one another about who is right
Let us come as broken people seeking Your healing

If we confess, You have promised to forgive us
If we seek Your face, You have promised to change us
As we see how powerless we are, we see how great You are

Please, Father, take Your gentle hands and move us toward
Yourself

[Not in your own strength]
for it is God Who is all the while effectually
at work in you [energizing and creating in you the power and desire]
both to will and to work for His good pleasure and
satisfaction and delight.
Philippians 2:13 TAB

THE SPIRIT OF THE LORD IS WITH ME

Oh Father, *thank You* that You're here with me
Holding my hand, loving me, changing me
Thank You that with Your loving kindness
You're melting all the bitterness in my heart
That Your God-light is shining into the dark corners of my mind
Searching out those secrets tucked away
Carefully hidden, nicely covered-over strongholds
Places the enemy has gotten his foot in the door
And carefully, quietly taken control of my thinking
Thank You that You're allowing me to see these things
Thank You that You're taking the time to change me
To mold me and make me into who You made me to be
Thank You that I don't have to be ashamed
As I stand naked before You
That I stand here covered in Your love and Your Son's blood
Thank You that You're refreshing my heart and purifying it
Please hold my hand as we go through this cleansing
Help me to allow Your blessed Holy Spirit
To cleanse me and change me into Your Son's likeness
Help me not to be afraid during this changing process
Help me to understand that my freedom is just a breath away
Help me to fight the enemy with Your Word
Your Son's name and His Blood
Help me to learn and grow strong in Your strength
So that I can help those who come behind me

Now this Lord is the Spirit, and where the Spirit of the Lord is, there is freedom. And we with our unveiled faces reflecting like mirrors the brightness of the Lord, all grow brighter and brighter as we are turned into the image that we reflect; this is the work of the Lord who is Spirit.
2 Corinthians 3:17-18 Jerusalem Bible

ENTER INTO HIS GATES
WITH THANKSGIVING
AND A THANK OFFERING
PSALMS 100:4 TAB

ALWAYS GIVE THANKS CHILD

GIVE THANKS, CHILD

Give thanks to Me, child, before you can see
Give thanks when the burden's too heavy to bear
Give thanks when you feel downtrodden
Give thanks when your heart's heavy with sorrows

Give thanks, because giving thanks sets you free
Give thanks, child, give thanks before you can see
Give thanks, because giving thanks sets you free

Giving thanks in everything, moves My hands
Giving thanks moves My heart and brings Me to your side
Giving thanks in and for everything is faith
Giving thanks, child, is called the sacrifice of praise

Give thanks morning, noon and night
Give thanks, child, you will see, it sets you free!

Always give thanks for everything to our God and Father
in the name of our Lord Jesus Christ. Ephesians 5:20 TLB

No matter what happens, *always be thankful.* For this is God's will
for you who belong to Christ Jesus. 1 Thessalonians 5:18 TLB

THANK YOU FOR WHAT MY EYES CAN'T SEE

Father, *how long do I thank You, when my eyes can't see*
A day, a month, a year, or only an hour?
How long, Father? How long does it take?
Please Father, give me a knowing, a knowing in the center of me
A knowing not built on sight but on trust
A thing that my spirit can touch
A faith in my God, who calls things into being
Things that our eyes can't see, but we know come from You
This is what I long for, this is my cry
Lift me up Father, wipe the tears from my eyes
Take my hand, and remove the fear from my heart
Help me to lead others in *thanking You for what our eyes can't see*

When everything was hopeless, Abraham believed anyway,
deciding to live not on the basis of what he saw he couldn't do
but on what God said he would do. . . .
He didn't tiptoe around God's promise asking cautiously skeptical
questions. He plunged into the promise and came up strong,
ready for God, sure that God would make good on what he had said.
Romans 4:18-20 The Message

69

I WONDER

I wonder, I wonder, I wonder
How long will it take
My mind shifts back through time
To Abraham, whom You loved so dearly
Chosen by You, led by You
I wonder what he thought
As he pondered Your promise
As the years went by
Year after year after year
No answer in sight
The times he turned from Your path
The fear, the mistakes he made
Trying to make the promise happen
By his own wisdom
And might
The years went by, so many of them!
The promise didn't come
His friends laughed
As he *thanked You* for the promise
They saw no answer
Still he turned his eyes toward You
Waiting, wishing You'd hurry
Hearing the laughter, and doubt
Yet believing, it seemed, against all hope
That You'd do what You said You'd do
Like Abraham, who believed
And so became the father of many nations
I too, stand here looking to You
Keeping my thoughts on Your promises
Thanking You, loving You
Waiting for my eyes to see
What my heart has heard

Against all hope, Abraham in hope believed and so became the father of many nations, Being fully persuaded that God had power to do what he had promised. Romans 4:18-21 NIV

IT'S TIME TO TRUST, CHILD

Child, look, turn, seek!
Its a time to trust when your eyes can't see
Its a time to remember what has gone on before
A time to cling to My promises like you never have
Its a time for wondering to cease
And praising to begin
Flowing over everything and everybody
To clasp the hand of your Father
To remember My promise
That I'll never leave you
That I'm always here
Waiting for you to grow
To bloom where I've planted you
You are My child, chosen from many
To speak of My wonders
To tell of My love
This is why I'm molding you
Taking the time to strip and cleanse you
So you can be used by Me

Give thanks to the LORD, for he is good!
His faithful love endures forever.
Psalms 107:1 NLT

LIFE IS NOT WHAT IT SEEMS

Father, I'm so happy that what it seems like
And what You say it is, are two different things!
I couldn't stand it if I only looked at what it looks like
But, praise Your Name, I don't have to look
at what my eyes can see
Like Abraham, I only have to look at Your promises!
Such joy, such overwhelming joy, such peace
Knowing that in faith I can turn my eyes to Your face
That I can see beyond what is to what Your Word says
Like Abraham, I too believe in a God who raises the dead
Who calls things that are not as though they were
Against all hope, I too can believe Your promises and so become
I too can sing and praise before I see the answer!
I too can dwell in Your unspeakable joy--called faith
Thank you for what I can't see, Father; praise Your Mighty Name
I love You so much!

Now faith is the substance of things hoped for,
the evidence of things not seen. . ..
But without faith it is impossible to please him:
for he that cometh to God must believe that he is,
and that he is a rewarder of them that diligently seek him.
Hebrews 11:1-6 KJV

I WILL BELIEVE !

I will
Praise the Lord
For what my
Eyes can't see
And my ears
Can't hear
But my
Heart Knows the Truth of
Even though
It looks like
It will never happen
I will still
Believe
Because I
Believe in a
God who
Raises the dead
And calls
Things
That are not
As though they were
Like Abraham I too
Will believe
And so
Become

❖ ❖ ❖

Abraham never wavered in believing God's promise. In fact, his faith grew stronger, and in this he brought glory to God. He was absolutely convinced that God was able to do anything he promised. And because of Abraham's faith, God declared him to be righteous. Now this wonderful truth--that God declared him to be righteous—wasn't just for Abraham's benefit.
It was for us, too, assuring us that God will also declare us to be righteous if we believe in God, who brought Jesus our Lord back from the dead. He was handed over to die because of our sins, and he was raised from the dead to make us right with God. Romans 4:20-25 NLT

ENTER INTO HIS GATES WITH THANKSGIVING

Father, in the quiet of the morning I come to Your feet
I'm here to worship You, to love You, to talk to You
When I think of the love You Have for me, I'm overwhelmed
Overwhelmed that You, Father, Who made heaven and earth
Care about me, that You take the time to instruct me
That You Yourself are my teacher, makes any lesson good

Father, I'm amazed how You're changing my heart
How Your eyes continually search my inner being
Sorting things, pulling things out, touching
spots with Your healing
Abba Father, *thank You* for loving me, *thank You* for making me
Thank You for using me to express Your love to others
Thank You, Father! Thank You! Thank You! Thank You!

Enter into His gates with thanksgiving and a thank offering
and into His courts with praise!
Be thankful and say so to Him, bless and
affectionately praise His name!
For the Lord is good; His mercy and loving-kindness are everlasting,
His faithfulness and truth endure to all generations
Psalms 100:4-5 TAB

ALL THINGS WORK TOGETHER

Dear Father God
I just want to tell you *thank you*
***Thank you* for my life**
From my beginning day, to this day
And for every day that is to come
There are things I wish had never happened
And things I hope to never have to face
There have been the good and wonderful things
Love and happiness, joy and peace
I want to take this opportunity to *thank you*
For never leaving me or forsaking me
For walking with me
Through the good and the bad times
I just want You to know that I'm beginning to understand
That nothing has ever happened to me
That You have not allowed to happen
Each and everything has had a purpose
And I stand on the Word that says
All things will work together for my good
Because I love you so much

And we know that all that happens to us is working for our
good if we love God and are fitting into his plans.
Romans 8:28 TLB

WAITING

Father how come it takes such
A long, long time
For you to answer some prayers?
How long will the waiting be?

Sometimes it takes
A long time, child
Because you don't
Hear what I'm saying
You only see what
You want Me to do

You never hear
What I'm asking of you
How hard will you seek My face?
How deep will you search
For Me and My answers?

So take my hand, child
As we climb this climb
It will draw you closer to Me
Then you've ever been

For since the world began no one has seen
or heard of such a God as ours,
who works for those who wait for him!
Isaiah 64:4 TLB

THANK YOU!!

Good morning, dearest Father
Thank You, thank You!
For this day, for my life
Thank You, Thank You!
For the buckets of love
You pour over me and mine

Thank You for sending Your Son
For the world!
For giving all people
Hope of eternal life with You!
JESUS is the way!
JESUS is the price paid!
JESUS is our sacrifice!
JESUS is the living Son of God!!

Thank you, thank You, Thank you!

Let them offer *sacrifices of thanksgiving* and
sing joyfully about his glorious acts.
Psalms 107:22 NLT

But I will give *repeated thanks* to the Lord,
praising him to everyone.
Psalms 109:30 NLT

THANKS FOR BEING MY FATHER

Father, thanks **for being my Father**
Thanks **for filling that empty spot**
Filling it with Your love and kindness
With Your compassion and understanding
With Your wisdom and knowledge

Thank You **for pouring Your love out on me**
Thank You **for speaking through me**
Thank You **for loving through me**
Thank You, Father, **for everything You are!**

Enter with the password: *"Thank you!"*
Make yourselves at home, talking praise.
Thank him. Worship him
Psalms 100:4 The Message

THE WASHING

Father, thank You
For washing our minds
With the water of Your Word
For daily cleansing us
And changing us
For releasing us from the past
For loving us into the future
For being the Light
That guides us
Down Your way
Thank You, thank You, thank You
We love You so much!

I love you, too, children
You give me joy!

Don't copy the behavior and customs of this world, but let God
transform you into a new person by changing the way you think.
Then you will know what God wants you to do,
and you will know how good and pleasing and perfect his will really is.
Romans 12:2 NLT

LEAVE IT AT MY FEET, CHILD

Father, what if we have something
Sad or bad to talk over with You?

Of course, child, bring it to Me, talk it over with Me
Then leave it at My feet, and go on about your business
Praising Me for the answer you can't see
Thank Me in advance for your heart's desire

Don't forget to remember that I'm GOD!
That My way might not always be your way
But *you must thank Me anyway*
Thank Me that I love you, that I'm holding your hand
That I'm walking each step of your life with you
Child, speak words of love, words of *thanksgiving*
MY WORDS, child, MY WORDS!

And don't forget to give Me praise, and *thanksgiving*
From the rising of the sun to the setting of the sun
Even through the nights, when you're awake or asleep
This is My desire, child, this is My command
PRAISE ME, LOVE ME, *THANK ME,* OBEY ME!
These things will open the flood gates of Heaven
And My blessings will pour out upon you and yours
Try Me, child, please try Me

Blessed be the name of the Lord
From this time forth and forever.
From the rising of the sun to its setting
The name of the Lord us is to be praised!
Psalms 113:2-3 NASV

I Will Pour My Spirit Upon Your Offspring,
And My Blessing Upon Your Descendants. And
They Shall Spring Up Among The Grass Like
Willows Or Poplars By The Watercourses.
One Will Say, I Am The Lord's; And
Another Will Call Himself By The Name
Of Jacob; And Another Will Write [Even
Brand Or Tattoo] Upon His Hand, I Am The
Lord's, Thus Says The Lord,
The King Of Israel And His Redeemer,
The Lord Of Hosts:
I Am The First And I Am The Last; Besides
Me There Is No God.
Isaiah 44:3b-6a NASV

YOUR CHILDREN
ARE MY CHILDREN

OUR WATCH CARE

We watch our children grow
From a small tiny seed
Surrounded by our body
Surrounded by our love
Given to us as ours
To cherish, to love
To cuddle and protect

Oh the joy, the love, the tenderness
The holding of the little hands
The leading, the guiding, the praying
The implanting of wisdom
The fear of what we might miss
As we lead and teach them
As we walk with them through life

Oh the joy they bring
As we help them conquer their small world
Watching them running and playing
Joy in their hearts, songs on their lips
Laughter in their eyes
Thinking we're so fortunate they're ours
Such a gift from God
Thank you so much, Father

May all the gifts and benefits that come from God our Father, and the Master, Jesus Christ, be yours. 1 Corinthians 1:3 The Message

For I will pour water on the thirsty ground and send streams coursing through the parched earth. I will pour my Spirit into your descendants and my blessing on your children. Isaiah 44:3 The Message

So thank GOD for his marvelous love, for his miracle mercy to the children he loves. Psalms 107:31 The Message

GIVE THEM TO ME, CHILD

What do You mean, Lord? How do I let go?

Bring your family and hand them to Me

But it seems I'm stuck to them like glue
I just don't know how to do this, Father

Child, you get up in the morning and bring them to Me
Then get on with your day
You must praise Me *and thank Me*
For all the things your eyes can't see

This is called faith, child
It must come from the heart
It must be honest and true
You must look into My face
And know these are the things I will do!

I'm able to speak to their spirit from the inside out
I'm able to make them desire Me, to sing and shout
Let go child, I LOVE THEM MORE THAN YOU DO!

God is not a man, that he should lie,
nor a son of man, that he should change his mind.
Does he speak and then not act? Does he promise and not fulfill?
Numbers 23:19 NIV

FANATICAL

You know, Father, my kids and grandkids young and old
Think I'm fanatical about You
Why, she couldn't even eat a piece of pie
Without saying it came from You
I'm sure my husband often thinks this, too
Why does this surprise me?
When I've cried, Lord, teach me more!
I don't care if people think I'm fanatical!
Let me be consumed by my Love for You!
And most of all Your love for me!
They think I'm overboard
And wonder why I won't quit
But, Father, how can I quit
When I only want to have more of You?
What am I doing Lord?
Am I pushing them away?
When I'm only trying to draw them closer to You
I'm getting tired, Lord
What shall I do, how can we all be free?
Then from the center of my being comes the whisper
Just give them back to Me child, please

God--you're my God! I can't get enough of you!
I've worked up such hunger and thirst for God.
Traveling across dry and weary deserts.
Psalms 63:1 The Message
Jehovah is our God, Jehovah alone. You must love him with all
your heart and soul, and might. And you must think constantly
about these commandments I am giving, you today. You must
teach them to your children and talk about them when you are at
home or out for a walk;
At bedtime and the first thing in the morning.
Deuteronomy 6:4-8 TLB

GIVE THEM BACK TO ME, CHILD

I love you child, just give your family back to Me
I love them so much more than you do
I've only loaned them to you
To love and nurture, to kiss and hug
To train up in the way they should go
To teach them of My love
To watch over them and protect them
You will kiss away their hurts
When you can't make the hurts go away
You will hold them, you will cry and grieve with them
You will fight their battles with them
And you will rejoice in their victories
In the good times you will laugh and rejoice with them
You will sing them songs about Me
You will dance for joy with them
You will tell them about Me
Who I am, and how I love them
So they can see me and love Me as you do
You will tell them of my joy in them, of My great love for them
You will tell them, train them, teach them about Me
Again and again you will tell them about Me
You will live your life about Me
You will show them Me
And so comes that moment when we take our most precious gifts
From the center of our being we hand them back to You
Thank you for giving us the responsibility of raising Your children
Forgive us our failures and mistakes
Thank you for standing in the gap for us
Please help us, Father, as we raise these children, that You've loaned us

So *thank GOD* for his marvelous love,
for his miracle mercy to the children he loves.
Psalms 107:31 The Message

I'M AFRAID, FATHER

Father, I'm asking for directions
What can I do for my children?

Take your hands off of them, child
Let Me handle this; I know what I'm doing
Hide in Me, pray constantly, fast
Bind them to Me, and *give thanks without end*

I feel afraid, Father
I know you do, child
Sit here at My feet and rest
Keep your eyes on My face
Lean against Me
All will be well

Father--
Yes child?
I love you
I love you too, child

But the Lord says, "Even the captives of the most mighty
and most terrible shall all be freed; for I will fight those
who fight you, and I will save your children."
Isaiah 50:25 TLB

STRIVE OR TRUST?

Child-- yes Father?
Come and sit by My feet
Lean against Me
This is where the weary come to rest
You are wearing yourself out
With your striving and failures
Trying to think in a way that isn't from Me
Child, come up against Me
Let Me fill you with My peace and love
My joy and forgiveness
My nearness, My understanding
Let Me fill you with Myself
Come into My rest
Turn your face to Mine, put your hand in Mine
TRUST ME!
You can only trust Me
By being still in My presence
Let Me touch your heart
Let Me work in your people's hearts
Let Me show them Myself
Let Me show them Myself in you
None of this can you do yourself
It is My job, let Me do it
Your job is to sit at My feet and *give thanks*
Please Help me to understand this, Father

Thus we have been set free to experience our rightful heritage. You
can tell for sure that you are now fully adopted as his own children
because God sent the Spirit of his Son into our lives crying out,
"Papa! Father!" Doesn't that privilege of intimate conversation with
God make it plain that you are not a slave, but a child? And if you
are a child, you're also an heir,
with complete access to the inheritance.
Galatians 4:5-7 The Message

TAKE YOUR HANDS OFF THEM

Why Father? Why, must I let them go?
The ones I hold dear to my heart
The ones that are my life
You must take your hands off them
So you're all free to love Me
You must bring them to my feet, then walk away!
You must cut the cords of control
Remember the promises I've made to you, child
You have done your job
Now you must trust Me to do mine
I can't do it when your hands are in the way
Look in My face, child, keep your eyes on mine
Keep your hand in mine
I won't let you go, nor will I let them go
Bind them to Me with strong cords of love
Bind them to My wisdom
Look at Me, child, remember what your job is!
I've forgotten, Father, please tell me again!
Your job is to bind the enemy
Pray My presence into their lives
And give Me thanks, over and over again
For what your eyes can't see
Please child put a smile on your face
While you're doing this
Remember I'm the captain of this army
And I will stand guard over My soldiers
I love you child
Get on with thanking Me, and binding the enemy!

As the people began to sing and praise, the Lord set ambushes
against their enemies. II Chronicles 20:22 NIV

YOUR HANDS ARE IN MY WAY!!!

**Sit down child!
TURN! LOOK AT ME!
YOUR HANDS ARE IN MY WAY!!!**

*GIVE ME THANKS FOR WHATEVER
IS HAPPENING!!*

**Have you ever been able to stop anybody
From doing anything?**

I THINK NOT!

Bring it to me with thanksgiving and trust,
With faith in Me!

**CHILD, I'M TIRED OF TELLING YOU THIS!!!
For the moment
It's the only job I've given you!**

Always give thanks for everything
to our God and Father in the name of our
Lord Jesus Christ. Ephesians 5:20 TLB

**Please forgive me Father for taking so long to learn this truth
I know what Your saying is the TRUTH!
I will obey in Jesus name!**

WHAT TO PRAY, FATHER?

Father, help me please, I don't know what to pray!
What words will cover each situation?
What words shall I say, Father?
What words to pray over my family?

Speak what you want for them, child!
Write what you want for each one of them
Lay hands on the paper daily and pray in the Spirit
As you do this, the requests and *thanksgiving's*
Will be written on your heart and fall out of your mouth easily
Find Scriptures, write them with your requests
Then praise Me, *thank Me,* speak MY WORDS over your people
And see the things I will do, child!

Thank You, Father
That You will not leave these things undone!

Child?
Yes Father?
Do not worry any longer
About the way you pray
Do not desire other peoples words
The words you have, are the words I've given you
Do not desire their words child, it does not give honor to Me

Don't fret or worry. Instead of worrying, pray. Let petitions
and praises shape your worries into prayers, letting God know
your concerns. Before you know it, a sense of God's wholeness,
everything coming together for good, will come and settle you down.
It's wonderful what happens when Christ displaces
worry at the center of your life.
Philippians 4:6-7 The Message

MY PRAYER

Dearest Father God
Lover of me and mine
I hold out my hands
Palms up
To receive all
You have to give
I lift my hands
High to You
Trying to give You
All that I am
In Jesus' Name, I ask You
Reach down from heaven
Pour everything You are
On my family
Husband, sons and daughters
Grandchildren
Old and young
All my family
Here and there
Teach them of Yourself
Your goodness, Your greatness
Thank you, for Your great love for them!
Father, please draw them
To Yourself
Teach them to know You
To serve and love You
This is my desire of my heart!
Thank you
Thank You
Thank You!

Delight yourself in the LORD and he will give you
the desires of your heart. Psalms 37:4 NIV
O our God, *we thank you* and praise your glorious name!
I Chronicles 29:13 NIV

MY SAD, SAD HEART

Father, my heart is sad
My tears are ready to fall over things
That grieve You and I
Things I cannot change
But instead of crying
I turn my thoughts to You
I think of Your love
For me and mine
I think of all the promises You've given me
All the instructions
You've so carefully laid before me
To cover us all with Your Son's Blood
To bind our minds to Yours
You say "pray and *give thanks*, child
Based on My promises
Before your eyes see
Trust Me, believe I love you all
And I'm working in your lives
So, Father, even though my heart is sad
As I turn my eyes to Yours
I feel the thickness
Of your peace surround me
I can return to my bed now
My eyes grow heavy
As I think on Your promises
Trusting You, praising You
Thanking You, over and over
And over, till sleep comes

So we Your people and the sheep of Your pasture
will *give thanks* to You forever;
To all generations we will tell of Your praise.
Psalms 79:13 NASV

NIGHT TIME REVERIE

Arise in the night and cry out for the lives of your children!
I hear Your whisper loud and clear
So here I am kneeling at Your feet
Laying my worries and fears on Your lap
Praising and *thanking You*
Turning my thoughts
Exchanging them for Yours

As my mind moves over each child and grandchild
My faith starts building protective hedges around them
IN JESUS' NAME!
I cover them with THE BLOOD OF JESUS!
I bring them one and all before Your throne
Putting You in remembrance of Your promises
Of YOUR WORD!
As if You would ever forget!
I THANK AND PRAISE YOU!
For mighty Angel Warriors watching over them
That they rest cradled in the circle of Your arms
Down through eternity
Generation, after generation after generation

Those who live in the shelter of the Most High will find rest in the shadow of the Almighty. This I declare of the LORD: He alone is my refuge, my place of safety; he is my God, and I am trusting him. For he will rescue you from every trap and protect you from the fatal plague. He will shield you with his wings. He will shelter you with his feathers. His faithful promises are your armor and protection. Do not be afraid of the terrors of the night, nor fear the dangers of the day, For he orders his angels to protect you wherever you go.
Psalms 91:1-5,11 NLT

ONCE AGAIN, COMES THE WHISPER

Our children are grown now
To soon, it seems
We wish we had longer to be with them
That we had more time to teach them things about life
More time to do all the things
We didn't have time to do
Just more time with them, Lord, that's what we want
Father, why is it so hard to let go of them as children
To let them be the adults we've raised them to be?

Then once again we hear Your whisper
It's time to give them to Me
You've done your job, child
Now let Me be their Father, eternally,
The rest is up to Me
Now I will hold them
I will kiss their hurts
I will rejoice in their victories
I will lead them down My paths
I will pick them up when they fall
I will love them beyond anything they can know

"And this is my covenant with them," says the LORD. "My Spirit
will not leave them, and neither will these words I have given you.
They will be on your lips and on the lips of your children and your
children's children forever. I, the LORD, have spoken!"
Isaiah 59:21 NLT

AS ALWAYS

Now they will be My children
Bearing My Name
Bearing the blessings of My Son's victory
I will walk with them
I will teach them to hear My still small whisper
I will rejoice with them, I will cry with them
I will lead them and train them
I will rejoice over them, as My sons and daughters

These are the things I will do, child
I wont leave them undone, I promise
Trust Me, I will be a good Father to them!
Give them to Me, child, trust Me!

So once again we loosen our life-giving grip
Cry a few tears, and place our children in Your large hands
Knowing it's the only way we can all be free
Deciding to enter this new phase of life, with joy
To share and rejoice in their adult lives
To not only be their much loved parents, but also their friends
Thank You Father, for sharing <u>Your children</u> with us!

What marvelous love the Father has extended to us! Just look at it-
we're called children of God! That's who we really are.
I John 3:1 The Message

"BE KIND AND COMPASSIONATE TO ONE
ANOTHER, FORGIVING EACH OTHER,
JUST AS IN CHRIST GOD FORGAVE YOU."
EPHESIANS 4:32 NIV

DRAW THE POISON FROM OUR WOUNDS

THERE COMES A TIME

There comes a time in everyone's life
When we must look into the depths of our soul
The sin and corruption we see there
Will astound us and give us grief untold

Please, Heavenly Father
When this time comes, give us eyes to see
Your loving kindness, Your forgiveness
Your mercy flowing deep and free

Finally, I confessed all my sins to you
and stopped trying to hide them.
I said to myself, "I will confess my rebellion to the LORD."
And you forgave me! All my guilt is gone.
Psalms 32:5 NLT

THROUGH MY FATHER'S EYES

Father, I'm tired of seeing myself
Through my own eyes
Or through the eyes of the condemner
The accuser, the liar!
Please, Father, let me see myself
Through Your eyes
Eyes that love me unconditionally
Eyes that made me
Healing eyes that see me, as no one else sees me
Only You can show me who I really am in You
Only You can show me how to love myself
Only You can show me my great worth to You
Only You can cut away the things of the past
Only You can set me free
Only You can give me a new picture of myself
Only You can show me
That I'm really free
Only You can show me what it means
To be covered in Your Son's sacrifice
Child, you stand before me in flowing garments
Of My Son's crimson blood
That's how precious you are to Me
I gave My Son for you
How I love you
How tenderly I watch over you
Look into My face, child
I'll be happy to teach you this truth

You are a chosen race, a royal priesthood, a dedicated nation
[God's] own purchased, special people, that you may set forth
the wonderful deeds and display the virtues and perfection's of Him
Who called you out of darkness into His marvelous light.
1 Peter 2:9 TAB

YOU MUST FORGIVE AS I'VE FORGIVIN YOU

As I look out the window
At the crisp and frosty view
Suddenly it reminds me
Of the quiet unforgiveness
Lodged in my cold and frozen heart
As I sit thinking of Your words
You must forgive, as I've forgiven you
The sun slowly rises
Casting it's glorious sunbeams
Across the lake melting and thawing
Bringing warmth to the land
Thank you Father
That as I ask you to forgive me
And allow You to forgive others through me
My heart is also thawed by the love of Your Son
And that by my obedience to Your Word
I am set free of my cold and frozen heart
Thank You for bringing
The warmth of Your love to my life

Now I will sing out my *thanks* to the Lord!
For though I was poor and needy,
he delivered me from my oppressors.
Jeremiah 20:13 NLT

UNFORGIVNESS

Father, why does it hurt so much?
How can we bear the pain?
Why in the middle of grief and anger
Do we always hear Your whisper,
"You must forgive, child as I've forgiven you"
How can you expect this of us, Father?
Why do You gently, but strongly demand this of us?
What is so important about forgiveness?

Child, without forgiveness you can never be free
Free to love others with My love
Unforgiveness clogs the path that love takes
It twists and corrodes your mind
It's rancid and it burns on the inside
Your heart gets hard and won't function right
This goes on for a lifetime
Until you let the pain and hurt go
Until you can give Me the anger and bitterness
Until you let My forgiveness flow through you

Trust me, child, I'll show you the way
One step at a time

For if you forgive people their trespasses (their reckless and willful
sins, leaving them, letting them go, and giving up resentment)
Your heavenly Father will also forgive you.
Matthew 6:14 TAB

SEEDS

Hidden deep in our souls
Are tiny seeds
Seeds of unforgiveness
Planted there by the enemy
Carefully covered over with layer after layer
Of justification and bitterness
Not knowing what to do with it
Or how we will survive
We strive to bury it
Trying to hide our rejection
Our shame, our deep hurt, our broken heart
Our fear of repetition, the shock of our loss
Our anger over the things that were taken from us
Trying to get on with life, instead of dealing with it
We've planted it as deeply as we can
And carefully covered it over
With layer after layer
Of anything we can think of that helps us
survive our hurt and fear
Thinking we've hidden it and put it to rest
At least for most of the time
When in reality what we've done is to plant it!
Not knowing that it is growing larger and larger
The roots reaching out to entangle the rest of our lives
Sucking and pulling the very life and joy from us

Then comes the whisper, "Forgiveness, child
You must forgive as I've forgiven you

Be kind and compassionate to one another, forgiving each other,
just as in Christ God forgave you.
Ephesians 4:32 NIV

COULD YOU WASH THE FEET OF JUDAS?

Help us to understand, Father, that this is possible
Help us to know that with Your strength and power
We can kneel at the feet of our enemies and wash their feet
The ones who've hurt us, the ones who've shamed us
The ones who have rejected us and deeply harmed us
To wash their feet, to tell them of Your love
To set <u>them</u> free, from our everlasting unforgiveness
Help us to understand that by this act of love
That by humbling ourselves and washing their feet
By loving them with Your love, is the only
way that <u>we</u> can be free

Take my hand, Father, turn my eyes to Your face
And show me these things I haven't been able to see
Another step towards higher ground
Thank You, Father, for walking with me

I'm telling you to love your enemies.
Let them bring out the best in you not the worst.
When someone gives you a hard time,
respond with the energies of prayer,
for then you are working out of your true selves,
your God-created selves.
This is what God does. He gives his best.
Matthew 5:44 The Message

UNFORGIVNESS AND JUSTIFICATION

Unforgiveness and justification
Go hand and hand
Oh how deep those roots grow
They tangle and entwine
Twisting their way through our lives
Growing deeper and deeper
Into the soft soil of our hearts
Twisting and turning, burrowing
Until our heart is no longer soft
It is hardened and out of shape
By unkind words and pains
A heart filled with
Hurts, lies, wrong thinking
Consequently we justify
Our own wrong behavior
Assuming that our thinking is right
So of course it must be the others that are wrong
Please help us, Father
To pull these life-destroying roots out
And be free!

(Now having received the Holy Spirit and being led and directed
by Him) if you forgive the sins of anyone, they are forgiven, if you
retain the sins of anyone they are retained. John 20:23 TAB

You must make allowances for each others' faults
and forgive the person who offends you.
Remember, the Lord forgave you, so you must forgive others.
Colossians 3:13 NLT

CHILD, I LOVE YOU

Child, I have come so that you can have life abundantly!
To live life bound up in lies and hurts is not an abundant life
An abundant life is a life of freedom
My Son paid a tremendous price for that freedom
My joy is that you should come to me
To recognize that I am your way to freedom
Child, look in My face
I am right here beside you
I will walk you through this
Day by day, minute by minute
You will begin to see the freedom
It will come about slowly,
But it will be real and you'll know it
Child, I love you!
Bind your heart and mind to My heart and mind
Lose this wrong thinking and let it go in Jesus' name
And watch your heart grow softer each day

The thief comes only to steal and kill and destroy;
I came that they may have life, and have it abundantly.
John 10:10 NLT

I CAN'T FORGIVE!

You struggle, you cry
I can't forgive! you say
I see no reason to try!
Why do I have to forgive?
When they are the ones in the wrong!
They are the ones who hurt me!
Who ripped my heart apart!
Who destroyed part of me!
Who covered me with fear and scars!
Why? Why me?
Why do I have to forgive?

And whenever you stand praying,
if you have anything against anyone,
forgive him and let it drop (leave it, let it go),
in order that your Father Who is in heaven may also forgive you
your [own] failings and shortcomings and let them drop.
Mark 11:25 TAB

CHILD, YOU MUST FORGIVE!

Child, come here, let Me hold you
Let me explain it to you once more
Forgiveness is so important
That I let my Son pay for your forgiveness
With His very life, His blood
His humiliation, His grief and sorrow
How often you forget this, child
He gave His life
So that you could live with Me forever
So that you could be free
Remember what I've told you about unforgiveness
How it ties you up in knots
So you can't function
You become hard and bitter
You try to cover your hurt with justification
There is only one way to be free of the torment
You must give it to Me
Let Me walk the path of forgiveness with you
So that you may learn to walk in
My love and forgiveness
Child, it's My way
There is no other way to have My peace and freedom
Come on, child, let's walk!
I will be with you each step of the way

Be gentle and forbearing with one another and, if one has a
difference (a grievance or complaint) against another, readily
pardoning each other's even as the Lord has [freely] forgiven you,
so must you also [forgive]
Colossians 3:13 TAB

FORGIVE US, FATHER WE KNEW NOT WHAT WE DID

As I drive down the road I see an old lady, holding a sign
"Babies Killed Here" the sign reads. That's pretty harsh
It sounds much better to use the word "abortion," it's calmer
To most it doesn't really seem like murder
Most of the time you don't even think of it like that
Mostly you're just plain scared, full of shame and fear
You don't know which way to turn, you don't know what to do
You feel like an animal in a trap, not knowing how to escape
You muddle through the options that your eyes can see
To marry someone who's so young he doesn't
even know what love is
To carry the child forever, to begin to love it and
then give it away
To be too young to understand that to give it away is love
To be too young
To even understand or comprehend any of these things
A few minutes at the doctor's and life goes on—
Normal for some, heartache and sorrow for others
Whichever the case
The day comes for all, when you must face your Maker
You must confess and repent and tell Him your grief
Then He gently reaches out and touches you with His Spirit of love
His Spirit of forgiveness surrounds you and you are washed clean

Let there be tears for the wrong things you have done. Let there be
sorrow and sincere grief. Let there be sadness instead of laughter,
and gloom instead of joy. Then when you realize your worthlessness
before the Lord, he will lift you up, encourage and help you.
James 4:9-10 TLB
The Lord is close to those whose hearts are breaking; he rescues
those who are humbly sorry for their sins. Psalms 34:18 TLB

HOW GREAT YOU ARE, LORD

How great is your love for me
So great that You continually
Keep reminding me of Your love and forgiveness
That You never let up day by day for a lifetime
Step by step, lesson by lesson
Thank You that when we have forgiven and adjusted to it
You then show us that there is an even a deeper level
So we go on, until time and obedience bring us
To a place where Your love and blessing
Can flow out through us onto the ones who've hurt us
Thank You Father for healing us
And setting our tormentors free

Thank you, again
That You take the time to walk with us
On this life-freeing journey

You're welcome, child

(Now having received the Holy Spirit, and being led and directed by Him) if you forgive the sins of anyone, they are forgiven, if you retain the sins of anyone, they are retained.
John 20:23 TAB

So (instead of further rebuke, now) you should rather turn and (graciously) forgive and comfort and encourage (him), to keep him from being overwhelmed by excessive sorrow and despair.
II Corinthians 2:7 TAB

TO KNOW WHAT IS RIGHT TO DO AND NOT DO IT

Father, Your Word says
"To know what is right to do and not do it is a sin"
I feel like I live in a cesspool of sin
Made up of piles and piles of little sins
Piled one upon another
Day after day after day, year after year
Not reading my Bible, not spending time with You
Eating something that's not good for me
Choosing the O.K. instead of the best
Not writing that encouraging letter
Not reaching out with a call
Sitting in front of the T.V. too long
Instead of doing something constructive
Whimpering instead of praising
Being fearful instead of trusting
Not making it to church for one reason or another
Nagging instead of encouraging
Holding on to tight to things
Not being organized, etc. etc. etc.
These are the small sins that are dragging me down
The ones I never think to ask forgiveness for
The ones I think I ought to be able to do myself
So they lay piled up on each other
A great accumulation as time goes by
Until the pile is so high I can hardly move about
Encompassed greatly by this hoard
Of small minute sins that suck me down
Down, down, down, so I can hardly reach You
Can hardly hear You, can hardly feel Your great love
Please help me, Father, as I wallow in my world of
To know what is right to do and not do it sins!

So any person who knows what is right to do but does not do it,
to him it is a sin. James 4:17 TAB

TO DO WHAT IS RIGHT

Child, as you look into My face
These things will slowly change and become natural for you
You will become quicker to ask My forgiveness in each of them
Asking forgiveness daily is one of the main things
You don't have to categorize each and every one
For fear that you will miss one
Just come to Me in sincerity and in love, not in fear
Come to Me child, My arms are wide open to receive you
My love is standing by to cleanse you of these things
I sent My Son Jesus to pay for your sins big and small
Once in a lifetime sins, as well as everyday sins

That you should even become aware of them is a good start
That you are talking to Me about them is even better
Yes, the pile gets very heavy and tries to bog you down
But I'm always here to take those sins
And to replace them with My peace!
I love you so much, child
It only takes a small time here and there to have a relationship
What we want is a day-by-day running relationship
One that never ceases
In that kind of relationship these sins fall off
As we walk along day by day, minute by minute
I love you child, come close to my heart
Let Me carry these burdens; take My peace in exchange, Please!
Just draw near to Me, child
That's the answer

Blessed be the Lord, Who bears our burdens and carries
us day by day,
Psalms 68:19-20 TAB

DRAW THE POISON FROM OUR WOUNDS

I sit here bathed in the morning light
A new dawn has begun
An era of forgiveness
A time of healing, a time of refreshing
Walk on with us, Father
As You renew our minds, and refresh our thoughts
Turn our faces towards You
Hold our hands in Yours
Draw the poison from our wounds
Placed there by time and the enemy
Pull out the roots, cleanse those wounds with Your love
Pour in the oil of Your healing
Give us eyes to see differently
And a heart filled with Your love
Reach YOUR arms out through us
And draw our brothers to Your heart
Help us, as we stand united in You
As we stand shoulder to shoulder
Forming a battle line
A line of safety and protection, around the lost
Help us to stand the stand
And fight the battle in Your Name
As You draw the lost into our family
Teach us to turn our time and energy
To fighting the real enemy

Then we your people, the sheep of your pasture, *will thank you forever* and ever praising your greatness from generation to generation. Psalms 79:13 TLB

ANOTHER OPPORTUNITY

**I shall consider this another opportunity *to give thanks*
Before I see the answer
I will not shiver and quiver in fright
I will look you in Your face
And dwell in the presence of Your grace**

The Lord is my strength, my shield from every danger.
I trust in him with all my heart.
He helps me, and my heart is filled with joy.
I burst out in songs of Thanksgiving.
Psalms 23:7 NLT

My Grace Is Enough;
It's All You Need.
My Strength Comes
Into Its Own In Your Weakness.
2 Corinthians 12:9 The Message

THE INS AND THE OUTS OF THE FAILURE PIT

THE DISAPPOINTMENT OF ME

Here I am again at the bottom of the spiritual slide
How did I slip and fall so easily?
How did You become God instead of Father?
Why did I fall instead of climb higher?
Why am I so tired and discouraged with me?
Why? Why? Why?

Shake me and toss me into the corner
Like an old doll you're ready to throw away!
Her body lumpy and out of shape
Her use, used up!
Her days numbered

The LORD himself goes before you and will be with you;
he will never leave you nor forsake you.
Do not be afraid; do not be discouraged.
Deuteronomy 31:8 NIV

CHILD, YOU ARE NOT A DISAPPOINTMENT!

Shhh— child, listen!
What you're hearing
Is the whispered lie of the enemy!
You've allowed it to come over and over again!
Instead of stopping it with
My Word, My Son's blood!
With the authority I've given you!
You've let the liar drag you down
Till you feel as if there's no up
IT'S A LIE, CHILD!
You know how important you are to Me!
You know I will never let go of you!
You know I will never let you be unusable to Me!
Now let Me help you up
Let's get on with what I've given you to do
Let's do it with MY strength and power!
Remember, I didn't pick you because you were so good at it
I picked you because I wanted to reach my people through you!
Oh yes, did you remember to ask My forgiveness
For the slippery ride you just took?
I love you, child!
Thank You, Father

But the Lord takes care of those he has forgiven.
Psalms 37:17b TLB

The steps of a good man are directed by the Lord.
He delights in each step they take. If they fall it isn't fatal,
for the Lord holds them with his hands.
Psalms 37:23-24 TLB

THE BLACK PIT

Feeling so low
Looking around at the things that are pulling me down
Failure here, failure there, failure everywhere
Why can't I overcome these things?
Even though there might be some truth in the accusations
Why does the enemy have to laugh so hard
As he kicks me, and stabs me with his pitchfork
With his black condemnation!
As he pushes me down, down, into his failure pit?
Wake up, child! Realize that it's a twisted lie!
Straight from the pit of hell!
Spoken to crush and destroy you!
To bring you harm!
To pull you farther and farther away from Me!
To wedge fear and condemnation in between us!
To surround you with lies!
To blanket you with fear and untruth!
Raise your head, child
Take My hand, look into MY eyes
See the great love I have for you
See My helping hand reaching out to you
Steady and calm, reaching, reaching down,
into your innermost being
Bringing My peace, My calmness, My love, My Joy
Instead of fear and condemnation
Oh Father, You're such an awesome God
You never leave me in the pit dug for me By the accuser
Thank You, thank you, thank You!

The thief comes only in order to steal and kill and destroy.
I came that they may have and enjoy life,
and have it in abundance (to the full, till it overflows).
John 10:10 TAB

HELP ME, FATHER!

Father, please help me here
Help me everywhere, I cry
What can I do without You?
NOTHING!

What can I do with You?
EVERYTHING!
So hold my hand
And show me Your way

Run Your strength
And power through me
Renew my mind
With Your Word

Change my thinking
Center my thoughts on You
Write Your Word in my heart
Help me to get into Your armor
Help me to make Your stand

Father, I'm here
Please hold my hand
Please produce the truth
Of Your Word in me!

I'm not saying that I have this all together, that I have it made.
But I am well on my way, reaching out for Christ,
who has so wondrously reached out for me.
Philippians 3:13 The Message

WHAT IS HAPPENING, FATHER?

Father, I was reading some of our letters recently
It seems as if they were from another time and place
A place faraway, a time long ago
I don't know how it happened or what happened
Just that a little crevice opened up between us
And I slowly slid in until...
I couldn't see Your face clearly
Even though I knew that
You were standing guard over me
I wasn't holding Your hand
It feels as if everyone is holding their breath
Waiting to see what has happened or is happening
Even I am in a state of limbo
Waiting, waiting to be changed into Your image
But bogged down by my sin and unconcern
Frozen in a passing moment of time
Wondering if it's all over
And I'll be left floating in space, never to be changed
What is this place we're in, Father?
Could you please tell me?

So here's what I want you to do, God helping you: take your
everyday, ordinary life--your sleeping, eating, going-to-work,
and walking-around life—and place it before God as an offering.
Embracing what God does for you is the best thing you can do for
him. Don't become so well-adjusted to your culture that you fit into
it without even thinking. Instead, fix your attention on God. You'll
be changed from the inside out. Readily recognize what he wants
from you, and quickly respond to it. Unlike the culture around you,
always dragging you down to its level of immaturity, God brings the
best out of you, develops well-formed maturity in you.
Romans 12:1-2 The Message

CHILD, CAN YOU HEAR ME?

Child?
Yes, Father?
Can you here Me?
Yes, Father

Child, look into My face
That is where the answers lie
It's just that you get so busy
You start thinking and meditating on so many things
The enemy really gets his foot in the door
Soon you don't remember who you are in Me
You don't remember who I am, You feel as if all is lost
But nothing is lost except your peace
Which only I can give
And give it I will!
If only you will relax and let Me love you
Hear My heart say, I love you

Child?
Yes Father?
Child, I love you so much!
Just come and sit by me all will be well
I promise!

Don't worry about anything; instead, pray about everything.
Tell God what you need, and *thank him* for all he has done.
If you do this, you will experience God's peace,
which is far more wonderful than the human mind can understand.
His peace will guard your hearts and minds
as you live in Christ Jesus.
Philippians 4:6-7 NLT

FATHER

Help! I can't be who You want me to be!
I keep looking away from Your face
I keep letting go of Your hand
Then I look around and I'm lost and scared
Full of anxiety, full of fear

How can I change? How can I make it?
How can I be what You want me to be?
There are so many things to change
So many things to do, so many people to reach
So many things to overcome and be better at
So many needs to meet, so many prayers to pray

Listen, Yahweh! Please, pay attention!
Can you make sense of these ramblings,
my groans and cries?
King-God I need Your help!
Psalms 5:1 The Message

CHILD

Come into My arms, child, let Me hold you
Don't be afraid, look into My face
Child, you must let Me be Your God.
Let Me be your everything

You keep forgetting to look at Me
You get lost in your failures
When all I want you to do is put them on My lap
Take your hands off them and dance away
Giving Me praise and *thanks*

Come, child, rest awhile
Sit on My lap while I hold you
Don't be afraid, just look into My face
I love you!
The changes that are coming will be fast and easy
Don't be afraid!

My grace is enough; it's all you need.
My strength comes into its own in your weakness
2 Corinthians 12:9 The Message

YOU ARE MY TREASURE

You have served me a lifetime, child
You have loved me as long as
You have known Me!
You never tire of telling others of Me
These are the things that count with Me
I love you, child; don't listen to the enemy
Don't let him pull and drag on you for so long
without coming to Me
Learn to recognize his black lies
Learn to recognize his form of terror and hopelessness
Learn to recognize him from afar
Don't let him get so involved with you
All your involvement should be with Me
You are My beloved child,
A child of the Almighty God

Remember, it's not by your strength, It never will be!
It is always My strength that I will run through you
My strength, child!
My strength that I will run through you!
My strength and power, child! My strength and power!

Take My hand; let Me help you out of that pit of lies
I love you so very much, it hurts Me
To see you covered with lies and discouragement
My precious child I love you
Come on, let's climb!

My dear children, let's not just talk about love; let's practice real
love. This is the only way we'll know we're living truly in God's
reality. It's also the way to shut down debilitating self-criticism,
even when there is something to it. For God is greater than our own
worried hearts and knows more about us than we do ourselves.
1 John 3:20 The Message

STOP TRYING TO BE

Child, stop trying to be anything
Look into My face
Take My hand
Concentrate on knowing Me
And My will
The other things
Will fall into place
By My will

Your only job is to look at Me
And to thank Me
And to praise Me
Before you see the answer

Then you will be free!
Free for Me to use you, as I please!
This is the truth you're looking for, child!
Hang on; it's quite a ride!

Do not despise this small beginning,
for the eyes of the Lord rejoice to see the work begin.
Zachariah 4:10 TLB

EMBRACING THE TRUTH

Father
When I think I can't do anything
That I can't complete the tasks
You've set before me
When they look impossible to me

I will loose these wrong patterns of thinking
From myself
Send them screaming down the garbage shoot
I will embrace the truth of Your Word
Craving it, receiving it from within

Binding myself to You
With strong words of love
Moving and swaying to the rhythm of Your heart
Knowing that I've found
A new place to start

As you learn more and more how God works, you will learn how to do your work. We pray that you'll have the strength to stick it out over the long haul----not the grim strength of gritting your teeth, but the glorious strength God gives. It is strength that endures the unendurable and spills over into joy, *thanking the Father* who makes us strong enough to take part in everything bright and beautiful that God has for us.
Colossians 1:9-11 The Message

DYING TO SELF

I sit along side Your feet
Bound to You with strong cords of love
Stillness pervades my spirit
And is entering my soul
I feel Your hand on my head
I am at peace…

You have said
That this is where the weary come to rest
Weary from the pursuit of freedom
From chasing change and obedience
Weary at failing

So I come to You in stillness
Waiting instead upon You and Your timing
Your joy and peace
Your freedom and Your power

Waiting for You to do something or nothing
Whatever pleases You, Master

Be still and know that I am God:
Psalms 46:9 KJV

THE LORD YOUR GOD IS WITH YOU, HE IS
MIGHTY TO SAVE. HE WILL TAKE GREAT
DELIGHT IN YOU, HE WILL QUIET YOU WITH
HIS LOVE, HE WILL REJOICE OVER YOU WITH
SINGING.

ZEPHANIAH 3:17 NIV

THE LOVE OF GOD

GOD'S LOVE, WHO CAN KNOW IT?

Gods love, who can know it?
The hungry child being fed
The warm blanket for someone in need of it
The smile we give as we pass by
The burden of a friend shared
This is Gods love as we know it

A hand that is held in a time of need
Tears and laughter shared
Truth told in a gentle way
A prayer as strangers pass by
These are but a touch of God's love as we know it

The King will reply, "I tell you the truth,
whatever you did for one of the least of these brothers of mine,
you did for me." Matt. 24:40 NIV

LIFT A FALLEN BROTHER

Child, take the things that have hurt and bound you
Turn them around for someone else's good
Reach down in the muck and mire, child
Lift a fallen brother
Help him to get out
It will be My hands you use to dust him off
It will be My heart you use to love him
It will be My path you help him get back on

Help them to understand that the God
Who began a good work in them
Plans to continue it
Help them to see what their eyes can't see
Help them to stand on My promises, in faith
Help them, child
This is why I've put you here

I'm planning on building an army
Out of hurt and wounded people
Out of people who have been caught up in bondage
People who have been rejected by society
Who will remember where they came from
Before they knew Me
People who will know and recognize My grace
My love, My power

Reach down, child
Lift a fallen brother

Being confident of this very thing,
that he which hath begun a good work in you
will perform it until the day of Jesus Christ.
Philippians 1:6 KJV

GOD'S LOVE, WHAT IS IT?

God's love is far above and beyond what our hearts understand
What does it mean to put the other person first?
What does it mean to stand by a friend?
What does it mean to never be jealous or envious?
What does it mean to give up our rights, give up our way?
What does it mean to search for and believe the
best of each person?
What does it mean to endure long and hope for the best?
What does it mean not to be touchy or resentful
when we are hurting?
What does it mean to love your enemy, the one you should hate?
Child, what it means is, that this is My love
Love like this can only come from Me
You must bring all these things to Me
You must lay them at My feet
You must ask me to do these things through you
That's what it means, child, bring them to Me
And I promise I'll do them through you
Thank You, Father
That You will love the people that You've put in my life
With a love that comes from You
Who dwells in the center of my being

God's love is-
...Very patient and kind, never jealous or envious, never boastful
or proud, never haughty or selfish or rude.
Love does not demand its own way. It is not irritable or touchy.
It does not hold grudges and will hardly even notice
when others do it wrong.
It is never glad about injustice, but rejoices whenever truth wins out.
If you love someone you will be loyal to him
no matter what the cost.
You will always believe in him, and always expect the best of him
and always stand your ground in defending him.
1 Corinthians 13:4-7 TLB

MY LOVE I POUR OUT ON YOU

I kneel at Your feet, Father
Thinking of how much I love You
In my hands I hold everything
I have and everything I am
Please accept my gift of love
As I lay myself and my things at Your feet
I turn and walk away, free
Free of my burdens
Free of my shortcomings
Free to be who You want me to be
A special child of God
Filled with the blessed Holy Spirit
Washed in Your Precious Son's Blood
Wrapped in Your love
What a wonderful tradeoff
Every thing I am
For every thing You are
I need You so badly
But isn't it strange that You somehow
Need all that I am and have?
Thank You so much

But the eyes of the Lord are on those who fear him,
on those whose hope is in His unfailing love
Psalms 33:18 NIV

By day the Lord directs his love,
at night his song is with me - a prayer to the God of my life.
Psalms 42:8 NIV

135

I LOVE YOU, CHILD

Father, I want to know You better
I want to see You clearer, not through a glass darkly
Give me love, Father, give me love that I can see
Child, My love reaches higher than you can see
It's wider than your mind can comprehend
It's deeper than you can know
My love for you, child, grows and grows
There is no end to My love for you
It's beyond anything your heart can know
I will fill you to overflowing, I will surround you
I will wrap you in a blanket of My love
I will hide you under my wings in the secret place
I will stretch out My huge arms over you There's never a place
or a moment that you'll be out of My sight
My love for you is something beyond your understanding
But I will give you all the knowledge of it that you can hold
You are so precious to me
I desire your love every minute of every day
My Word says, you love Me, because I first loved you
If you could understand the truth of that
Then you would be totally consumed by Me
And you and I would be one
Never, never would you feel alone again
You would be filled with Me, filled and running over
Everyone you touched would know my love
Are you ready for this kind of love, child?

May your roots go down deep into the soil of God's marvelous love;
and may you be able to feel and understand, as all God's children
should, how long, how wide, how deep, and how high his love really
is; and to experience this love for yourselves, though it is so great
that you will never see the end of it or fully know or understand it.
And so at last you will be filled up with God himself.
Ephesians 3:17b-19 TLB

I LOVE YOU, FATHER

I love You so much, Father
More than words can tell
You are my reason for living
You are my everything
You are my light, my joy

I bow my knees before You
I lift my hands to You
Father, love Yourself through me
So that I can be consumed by You

And you shall love the Lord your God
with all your heart and with all your soul
and with all your might.
Deuteronomy 6:5 NAS

YOU MUST LOVE YOUR FRIENDS AS THEY ARE

Child, you can't go on the praises of people
You are who I made you to be; you can't take the credit
If you do, it won't be worth a thing
I have made you a kind person, but remember, I made you this way
Not everyone will see you as I do
Standing in the Son's light, covered in garments of snow
Yes, this problem with friends has never happened before
For exactly as you said, I gave each one to you as a gift
I gave them to you because you chose Me
When you thought you'd lose them all
The reason I'm allowing this now is because I want you to grow
I want you to learn to be humble and gentle with your friends
I want you to make allowances for their faults
Because of your love for Me and My love for them
Do you understand, child?
I want you to learn to love your friends in
spite of their humanness
The same way I am teaching them to love you
Take my hand, child; it's just one more thing you'll
be so glad we did
My eyes are moving back and forth over your friendships
I am searching for people who want more of Me
I will fuse you together
So you can grow more than you thought possible
Do not keep chewing on and hassling over where you were wrong
Just seek Me and let me show you how to love
with unconditional love
To be a friend, you must love your friends as they are
Only I can help you do this, child

If you love someone you will be loyal to him no matter what the cost.
1 Corinthians 13:7 TLB

WHY ARE YOU SO SPECIAL ?

Who are you?
That He should send His Son to die for you
That He should bend down from Heaven
That He should scoop you up in His arms
Rocking you gently as you cry
Lifting you gently
Helping you to your feet
Touching your face
Saying, "Come on, child
I'll help you
We'll stand together
You and I"

Who are you?
That He would bend down and kiss your face
That He would dance with you
That He would let you touch His face
Are you someone special? Yes!
You're someone who knows that God loves them
Someone who's letting Him love Himself
And others through you
Letting Him love you
Through yourself and others
You are someone so special

In God's book
That's who you are!

God the Father chose you long ago,
and the Spirit has made you holy. As a result, you have obeyed
Jesus Christ and are cleansed by his blood.
May you have more and more of God's special favor
and wonderful peace. 1Peter 1:2 TLB

GOD IS A FATHER TO THE FATHERLESS

Father, look down on Your lost lambs
So many don't have fathers to guide them
Lacking that strong hand of leadership
The voice of wisdom leading the way
They've lost that covering that is so important
They wander out in the world alone, afraid
Some, because of this, won't understand Your Fathership role
Others will run to You in their great need of a Father
Father, please be to each lamb what they need

Child, I'm here; My eyes move back and forth over these lambs
My Spirit calls to them: "Come let Me be a Father to you
Come, let Me hold you, let Me carry your burdens
You don't have to be Fatherless anymore
Let Me be your covering, let Me be your life
Come little lambs, each of you mean the world to Me
Come little lambs, My yoke is easy and My burden is light"

He is a father to the fatherless;
he gives justice to the widows, for he is holy.
Psalms 68:5 TLB

He will feed his flock like a shepherd;
he will carry the lambs in his arms
and gently lead the ewes with young.
Isaiah 40:11 TLB

ABBA FATHER

Oh Father, I read in Your Word
Where You say Jesus was Your beloved Son
Your Son, chosen and marked by Your love
The delight of Your life, how fortunate for Him

And how fortunate we are, to be called children of God
To come, through Jesus, right up to Your throne
To be able to call You Abba Father, which means, Daddy
To climb up on Your lap, to be a delight to You
To be marked and surrounded by Your love

How can we ever *thank You* enough, Father?
I know! Now that I'm secure in being Your child
Now I can ask You to let me be Your servant

Because those who are led by the Spirit of God are sons of God.
For you did not receive a spirit that makes you a slave again to fear,
but you received the Spirit of sonship.
And by him we cry, "Abba Father."
The Spirit himself testifies with our spirit that we are God's children.
Now if we are children, then we are heirs—
heirs of God and co-heirs with Christ, if indeed we share in his
sufferings in order that we may also share in his glory.
Romans 8:14-17 NIV

CHILD, I DELIGHT IN YOU

Father, I love You more than words can say
Oh, how I love to hear You say, Child, I love you
There are no sweeter words to my ears
My spirit rejoices as I hear you sing over me
Child, I love you so, you are so dear to me

Father, I love you so much, take my heart
Draw me ever closer so that we become one
Consume me, so that my thoughts are Your thoughts
I throw my heart to the wind of Your Holy Spirit
Refresh me, set me on fire with a new, deeper love
A love for You that passes all human understanding
Father, I want more of You, fill me fuller
Bubble over on Your children, please use me

Child, I delight in you, I am filling you with Myself
I sing over you, because I love you
You are Mine, I am your God; I will walk
with you through eternity
I will give you a love for Me that surpasses human
understanding
I will make you mine, inside and out; you are My creation
Thank you for allowing Me to mold and form you as I planned
You are special to Me and I love you dearly

The Lord your God is with you, he is mighty to save.
He will take great delight in you, he will quiet you with his love,
he will rejoice over you with singing
Zephaniah 3:17 NIV

HELD SAFELY IN YOUR ARMS

How delightful to bask in Your love
To walk by Your light
To live in Your in presence
To relax in Your grace
How wonderful to be loved by God himself!
To be the apple of Your eye
The child of Your love
Held safely in Your arms
To be sung over by my God!
To always know You're watching me
Taking care of me
Leading me along Your path
This is too wonderful to believe
That I can never be lost to You!
Thank you for loving me!
Thank You for being my God!
Thank You, thank You, thank You!

Where can I go from your Spirit?
Where can I flee from your presence?
If I go up to the heavens, you are there;
if I make my bed in the depths, you are there.
If I rise on the wings of the dawn, if I settle on the far side of the sea,
even there your hand will guide me, your right hand
will hold me fast.
If I say, "Surely the darkness will hide me and the light become
night around me," even the darkness will not be dark to you; the
night will shine like the day, for darkness is as light to you.
Psalms 139: 7-12 NIV

143

TURN, CHILD, TURN

Turn, child, turn
Turn from self to Me
Seek My arms
Seek My face

Run, child, cling to Me; Turn from the world
Stay in the circle of My arms
You need nothing but Me

Turn, child, to Me and only Me
Your job is to look at Me
To love Me with all your heart
With all your soul and mind

Turn, child, hear My cry
There is very little you can do
In your own strength and power
But you can TURN TO ME!

Turn to face God so he can wipe away your sins,
pour out showers of blessings to refresh you.
Acts 3:19 The Message

SAFE AND SECURE IN YOUR ARMS

Father, here I sit, snug and warm
Watching the rain dripping and twirling
All that protects me are the walls around me
It's the same with Your love
I sit here in the midst of trouble and strife
Feeling safe and secure
Because Your arms are around me
Abba Father, I *thank You* for holding me
For loving me, for hiding me in Your secret place

You will keep in perfect peace
him whose mind is steadfast,
because he trusts in you,
Trust in the Lord forever,
for the Lord is the Rock eternal.
Isaiah 26:3-4 NIV

WORDS OF LOVE

Father, as I sit here thinking about You
Longing for new words
To tell You of my love

I watch, as I surrender myself
To the same familiar words
To the same old love phrases
My hands can't help but raise
Whether in thought or deed
"I love You, Father"
"Praise you, Father"

In my heart my knees bend in worship
Words of thanksgiving
Falling out of my mouth
"Thank you, thank you, thank You"

Thank You for my life, for the air I breathe
For the love You've given me
For the knowledge of my salvation
Thank You for the good and the bad times

Thank You that You're always with me
Thank You that You're my Father
Now and forever
Thank You, thank You
Thank You
What more can I say?

We thank you, O God!
We give thanks because you are near.
People everywhere tell of your mighty miracles.
Psalms 75:1 NLT

THE BEAUTY OF KNOWING YOU

The beauty of knowing You
Dwells deep inside of me
Down in the secret place
The place no one can touch
No one can see lest You
Show them You in me

I dance and sing
For love of You, My King
My heart overflows
As I sing Your song
My joy overflows in soft peacefulness

No one can take this knowledge
No one can steal Your love
I am surrounded by
The beauty of knowing and loving You
It's tucked safely away
In my heart

Most of what God does is love you.
Keep company with him and learn a life of love.
Observe how Christ loved us.
His love was not cautious but extravagant.
He didn't love in order to get something from us
but to give everything of himself to us.
Ephesians 5:2 The Message

147

Fear Not For I Am With You. Do Not Be Dismayed; I Am Your God. I Will Strengthen You; I Will Help You; I Will Uphold You With My Victorious Right Hand
Isaiah 41:13 TLB

CHILD, DON'T BE AFRAID

LOOK AWAY

Escape the pain and hurt--unknowingly look away
It's what I've always done, it's how I've survived
But look away to what?
Shopping, food, friends, books, controlling?
All of these things have taken my eyes off my problems
But, in turn, the answers have become the
problems, the addictions!

And so it goes, around and around, a circle without end
How do we break the circle? How do we get it under control?
When do we start and where do we stop?

The Master says, the answer lies in where you look
Don't look away, look into My face!
You've been looking in the wrong places, child
Take My hand, let's look into your heart

Not my heart, Master, I cry, this I cannot do!

Take My hand, child, we'll do it together, you and I

I try to pull my hand out of His, I try to look away
These are the secret things, Father
I've locked them up and cemented the door
They won't come open, no matter what I do!
I don't even want to look in there, Father, the fear I cannot bear!

Child, we need to look at the secret things in your heart
I need to pour My love into those hurting places, to heal them
We have to put My truth in there, so the circle can be broken

But how can I ever know what sins are lurking in my heart?
Cleanse me from these secret faults. Psalms 19:12 TLB

150

WHAT CAN I DO WITHOUT YOU?

Father, please help me here!
Help me everywhere I cry!
What can I do without You?
NOTHING!
What can I do with You?
EVERYTHING!
So hold my hand
And show me Your way

Run Your strength and power through me
Renew my mind, change my thinking
Center my thoughts on You
Write Your Word in my heart
Help me to get into Your armor
Help me to make Your stand

Father, I'm here, please hold my hand.
Please, produce the truth of Your Word in me!

So here's what I want you to do, God helping you:
Take your everyday, ordinary life--your sleeping, eating, going-
to-work, and walking-around life--and place it before God as
an offering. Embracing what God does for you is the best thing
you can do for him. Don't become so well-adjusted to your
culture that you fit into it without even thinking. Instead, fix your
attention on God.
You'll be changed from the inside out. Readily recognize what he
wants from you, and quickly respond to it. Unlike the culture around
you, always dragging you down to its level of immaturity,
God brings the best out of you,
develops well-formed maturity in you.
Romans 12:1-2 The Message

FATHER, WHERE ARE YOU?

Father, where are You? I can't find You!
I look for You in all the familiar places
But You don't seem to be there, where are You?
I can't see Your face, I can't feel Your hand in mine!

Things have gotten messed up
My life seems to be falling apart
Things I thought were secure aren't secure at all
Relationships I've tried to save are gone
My heart is hurt and crushed beyond repair
My mind is broken and I can't seem to fix it

Father, where are You?
Can't You see I need You?
I love You, Father, but I can't find You!
Did You leave? Are you mad at me? Have You forsaken me?
Help me, Father! Where are You?

I waited and waited and waited for GOD.
At last he looked; finally he listened.
He lifted me out of the ditch, pulled me from deep mud.
He stood me up on a solid rock to make sure I wouldn't slip.
He taught me how to sing the latest God-song,
a praise-song to our God.
Psalm 40:1-3 The Message

I HAVEN'T LEFT YOU, CHILD

Child! I'm here! I have never left you nor forsaken you
It is you who has left Me in your mind
You have assumed that because of the past
And because of your hurt and confusion, fear and sin
Your inability to cope, that I have left you
But I haven't left you, I've been here all the time
Child! Look at Me! You have served me a lifetime!
I know of your great love for Me, but child, there's more
You must know that I gave my only Son for you
With this knowledge comes freedom to live under grace
Freedom from the law, freedom from bondage and fear
Freedom to be accepted, just as you are!
Freedom to come into My presence, to come before My throne
Freedom to climb upon My lap, to sit at My feet
Freedom to call Me Abba, Father, to call Me Daddy
Freedom to leave the past behind to have a future
This is what I'm offering you, child
But it only comes through My Son's blood
Please take it, child, I love you so much
More than you could ever know
Please take it, child, come walk with Me
In a new and different way, I have the world for you
I have a future and a hope for you
Take my hand, child, come walk with Me

"For I know the plans I have for you," declares the
Lord, "plans to prosper you and not to harm you,
plans to give you hope and a future. Then you will call upon me
and come and pray to me, and I will listen to you."
Jeremiah 29:11-12 NIV

153

THE DESPAIR OF UNTRUST

Woe to the undoing of man as he lay in his bed
Covers over his head, lost in untrust and despair
How can he overcome it, who can he turn to?
Laxidazeness fills his soul, his mind, his will, his emotions
Taken over by the evil force, filling all the cracks and crevices
With fear and hopelessness, not knowing where to turn
What am I doing here? I who am a child of the King!
Despair is a dark and lonely place, filled
with unfair imaginations
What am I doing here?

God is love. When we take up permanent residence in a life of love,
we live in God and God lives in us. This way, love has the run of
the house, becomes at home and mature in us, so that we're free of
worry on Judgment Day—our standing in the world
is identical with Christ's.
There is no room in love for fear. Well-formed love banishes fear.
Since fear is crippling, a fearful life--fear of death, fear of judgment—
is one not yet fully formed in love.
1 John 4:16b, 17, 18 The Message
My dear children, let's not just talk about love; let's practice real
love. This is the only way we'll know we're living truly, living in
God's reality. It's also the way to shut down debilitating
self-criticism, even when there is something to it. For God is greater
than our worried hearts and knows more about us than we do
ourselves. We're able to stretch our hands out and receive what we
asked for because we're doing what he said, doing what pleases him.
Again, this is God's command: to believe in his personally named
Son, Jesus Christ. He told us to love each other, in line with the
original command. As we keep his commands, we live deeply and
surely in him, and he lives in us. And this is how we experience his
deep and abiding presence in us: by the Spirit he gave us.
1 John 3: 18-24 The Message

THE BATTLE OF DESPAIR

Pick up the paper
Pick up your pen
My Master says

The battle's not over
It's only begun
This battle of despair

Look the enemy in the eye
Don't forget the authority I've given you!
Don't give him an inch of grace

Recognize his fear!
Crush him with the Word of God!
With the Mighty Name of Jesus!

Grind him into the ground!
You are the Victor!
Never forget it!

Your victory was bought
With a mighty price
The spilled blood of your Savior

Don't let it be all for naught
Don't always lose
Because it seems too hard to do it!

Your fellowship with God enables you
to gain a victory over the evil one.
1 John 2:14b The Message

THE OTHER SIDE

Dearest Father, Lover of my soul
Thank You, thank You, thank You
I sit here on the other side of surgery
Amazed at everything You've done
Every little detail, not a thing overlooked
Nothing forgotten, nothing left undone

When I think of the torturous battle of fear and dread
I was caught in, hammered on by the enemy
Then I think of Your words, don't be afraid, child
Don't be afraid
I am with you; I will take care of you
I will uphold you with My mighty right hand
Over and over, whispered in my ear

It seems as if the only thing I could squeak out
Was thank you Lord, thank you for Your promises
Thank You for Your Word
Thank You before I see the answers

The LORD himself goes before you and will be with you;
he will never leave you nor forsake you. Do not be afraid;
do not be discouraged." Deuteronomy 31:8 NIV

But the LORD said to him, "Peace! Do not be afraid.
You are not going to die." Judges 6:22 NIV

When you lie down, you will not be afraid;
when you lie down, your sleep will be sweet. Proverbs 3:24 NIV

Peace I leave with you; my peace I give you. I do not give to you as the
world gives. Do not let your hearts be troubled and do not be afraid.
John 14:27 NIV

DIVINE POWER

Oh Father, *thank You* that You're right beside me
When I am quailing in fear, wincing from uncertainty
Thank You for Your patience as You move me along
Towards what You have always had in mind for me

Please forgive me for my stubbornness
For the strongholds in me, some set in place by choice
Some there from things beyond my control

Thank You that many are gone and mostly forgotten
Thank You that You're close to me, holding me, teaching me
As we embark on getting rid of the remaining ones

Thank You that You've made my mind sharp and clear
Full of Your Word and Your instructions for me

For though we live in the world, we do not wage war as the world does.
The weapons we fight with are not the weapons of the world.
On the contrary, they have divine power to demolish strongholds
2 Corinthians 10:3-4, NIV

DO NOT BE AFRAID!

Do not be afraid!
Do not be discouraged!
Your Word tells us this
Over and over and over
I wonder why
You tell us again and again?
Is it because You knew
That time after time
We'd be afraid and discouraged?
Is that why You sent Your Word?
To blanket us with Your love
To calm us, to prepare us
To help us understand
That You're always with us
That You hold us in
Your Mighty Right Hand
That You never leave us
Especially in times of trouble
That You are more than enough
The Great Comforter, our healer
That Your eyes are upon us
That You guide our steps
That You hold our hand
That You love us
More than we can ever know!
Thank You, Father!
That when I'm afraid
Or when I'm discouraged
I'll hear Your Voice whisper
Don't be afraid, child
I'm here, I'll never leave you

FEAR NOT for I am with you. Do not be dismayed I am your God.
I will strengthen you; I will help you; I will uphold you with my
victorious right hand.
Isaiah 41:13 TLB

THE JOURNEY

Casting my fears aside
I stride forward
Swinging, crushing, smashing
Strongholds in Jesus name
Ignoring cries of agony and fear
As walls come crashing down

Forcing myself to stand
Unaided by these life-long high walls
Smashing, crushing, destroying
Seeking my Father's face
As I move along toward freedom
And victory in Jesus name!

For God has not given us a spirit of fear and timidity,
but of power, love, and self-discipline.
2 Timothy 1:7 NLT

LIGHT OF MY LIFE

Father, You are the light of my life
Shining into the dark corners of my world
I am guided and directed by Your light
Sometimes I slip my hand out to cover it
Because I'm afraid of what we might see

You gently reach out and draw my hand down
Filling me with Your love and goodness
Flooding me with Your hope and revelations
Searching out the dark corners of my mind
Immersing me in the brightness of Your light

I stand lost in Your goodness and love
Covered by Your gentleness and kindness
Bathed in the warmth of Your healing light
Cleansing me, changing me into Your likeness
Thank You so much, Father!

You're welcome, child!

For God, who said, " Let there be light in the darkness,"
has made us understand that it is the brightness of his glory
that is seen in the face of Jesus Christ But this
precious treasure—this light and power that now shine within us—
is held in a perishable container, that is, in our weak bodies.
Everyone can see that the glorious power within
must be from God and is not our own.
2 Corinthians 4:6-7 TLB

DON'T BE AFRAID
OF THE LIGHT

**When the Son of God
Shines His light in your eyes
Don't cover them in fear
Throw your caution to the wind
Open wide your arms
Welcome Him, invite Him in
He's come to set you free
Dance and sing with your King
Love Him for all you're worth
Embrace His truths
Put on your garments of praise
Laugh and sing in the night
Join the ones who live in the light!**

I'm whistling, laughing, and jumping for joy;
I'm singing your song, High God. Psalms 9:2 The Message

Every bone in my body laughing, singing, "GOD,
there's no one like you !" Psalms 35:10 The Message

When the righteous see God in action they'll laugh, they'll sing,
they'll laugh and sing for joy. Sing hymns to God; all heaven, sing out;
clear the way for the coming of Cloud-Rider. Enjoy GOD,
cheer when you see him! Psalms 68:3,4 The Message

On your feet now--applaud GOD! Bring a gift of laughter, sing
yourselves into his presence. Know this: GOD is God, and God,
GOD. He made us; we didn't make him. We're his people, his
well-tended sheep. Enter with the password: *"Thank you!"* Make
yourselves at home, talking praise. *Thank him.* Worship him. For
GOD is sheer beauty, all-generous in love, loyal always and ever.
Psalms 100 The Message

FEAR OF THE UNKNOWN

What fights against fear of the unknown?
Faith in a Spirit God!
Why do we forget this?
Because He made us from dust
When will we remember?
When we've learned to recognize the enemy
And to put our God first
Above all other thoughts

That is why we can say with confidence,
"The Lord is my helper, so I will not be afraid.
What can mere mortals do to me?"
Hebrews 13:6 NLT

Surely God is my salvation;
I will trust and not be afraid.
The LORD, the LORD, is my strength and my song;
he has become my salvation." Isaiah 12:2 NIV

Then he continued, "Do not be afraid, Daniel.
Since the first day that you set your mind to gain understanding
and to humble yourself before your God, your words were heard,
and I have come in response to them. Daniel 10:12 NIV

SELF DEATH

Yea though I walk through the valley
Of the shadow of death
Death to life as I know it!
Death to self!
Death to wrong desires!
Death to my hiding places!

I will not be afraid!
For You are with me!
You hold me in Your arms!
But as I pour out my fear and sorrow
You allow me the knowledge
Of Your love surrounding me

Surely I am safe here
In the circle of Your arms
My eyes turned towards Your face
I hear You say
Give Me your hand, child
Lets climb!

…have compassion on us, and help us.
Mark 9:22 TLB

They Will Be Mighty Warriors For God,
Grinding Their Enemies' Faces Into The
Dust Beneath Their Feet. The Lord Is With
Them As They Fight;
Their Enemy Is Doomed.
Zachariah 10:5 TLB

PICK UP YOUR WEAPONS

THE EXCHANGE

Another day is here
The clock ticks off a new beginning
But Lord, the day has only begun
And I'm so tired already
So I take my tiredness and place
It on Your lap
I pick up Your robe of righteousness
The helmet of salvation
The shoes of peace
My pieces of armor set firmly in place
I exchange my tiredness
For Your strength
Come on, day
Let's get on the way

Last of all I want to remind you that your strength
must come from the
Lord's mighty power within you.
Ephesians 6:10 TLB

BINDING AND LOOSING

Binding and loosing
Binding and loosing
What do these words mean?

First, child
Binding yourself to Me
With strong cords of love makes sense
Where would you rather be
Than hooked on to Me?
Where would you be safer?
Where would you be more secure?
Nowhere else on earth or in Heaven
There is no safer or secure place to be
Than snug and tight against Me

Loosing is a step the other way
Where should the sin and pain go?
How about wrong thinking and strife
Bad words that are tied to you
With strong cords?
Let's loose them and strip them away
Lets loose them to go as far as they can
And never return
From the faraway land of the dead

I will give you the keys of the kingdom of heaven;
whatever you bind on earth will be bound in heaven,
and whatever you loose on earth will be loosed in heaven."
Matthew 16:19 and 18:18 NIV

A FIGHT TO THE FINISH

Child, look at Me! Concentrate on who I am!
Give Me thanks for the exact position you're in
It gives My hands permission to move on your behalf
What have I told you? That I will never leave you or forsake you
I am right here, standing alongside of you
Holding you, loving you, covering you
You know I am here
You know I love you, that I haven't forgotten you
I'm teaching you something, child, to fight a battle
This is the enemy that has held on the longest
This is the strongest one by far
But I'm in the middle of teaching you how to conquer
How to stand fast, how to be free
I'm not doing this for you, child
Because I love you
I'm teaching you how to do it
I'm right by your side, My hand in yours
My Son is in you, My Spirit is filling you, guiding you
Child, you have asked for My power
Before I give this gift, I must teach you how to use it
How to stand firm and wield the sword of deliverance
Don't be afraid; if you can't see Me clearly
Reach up and touch My face and you'll know I'm here

God is strong, and he wants you strong. So take everything the Master
has set out for you, well-made weapons of the best materials. And put
them to use so you will be able to stand up to everything the Devil throws
your way. This is no afternoon athletic contest that we'll walk away from
and forget about in a couple of hours. This is for keeps, a life-or-death
fight to the finish against the Devil and all his angels. Be prepared you're
up against far more than you can handle on your own. Take all the help
you can get, every weapon God has issued, so that when it's all over but
the shouting you'll still be on your feet. Truth, righteousness, peace, faith,
and salvation are more than words. Learn how to apply them. You'll need
them throughout your life. God's Word is an *indispensable* weapon. In
the same way, prayer is essential in this ongoing warfare.
Ephesians 6:10-17 The Message

HIGH TOWERS

Dearest Father God
Love of my life
Lifter of my heart
Respecter of my emotions
Even though often wrong
I give you my permission
I beg of You
Please help me
Crush and smash, tear down and
Grind into dust
The strongholds in my life
Help me to be free
Of the high towers
That have been built in me
I give my soul to You
My mind, will, and emotions
I also bring my wayward body
I ask You, Father
To bring them into alignment
Spirit, soul, and body
So all three are able
To bend down and worship Thee

Thanks and praises before I see

May God himself,
the God who makes everything holy and whole,
make you holy and whole,
put you together--spirit, soul, and body—
and keep you fit for the coming of our Master, Jesus Christ.
1 Thessalonians 5:23

SET MY CHILD FREE

The enemy comes to build high walls
Of regret and shame around us
To trap us in the webs of old hurts and deceit that he weaves
Hoping to bring us to the place in our minds
Where we think we are bound forever
With no way of escape

The enemy sits back with a smile
As he views his handiwork
Watching the tears roll down our faces
Thinking, I've got them now!

But he's forgotten one very important thing!
He's been messing with a child of the King!!

Our Father, King God speaks!!!
SET THEM FREE!!!!

I'll tear down the walls!
I'll wipe out the shame and regret!!
I'll unwind them from the web and set them free!!!
I'll dry their tears, and I'll turn their faces toward Me!!!!

"Not by might, nor by power,
but by my spirit," says the LORD Almighty. Zachariah 4:6 NIV

He is my strength, my shield, from every danger.
I trusted him and he helped me. Joy rises in my heart
until I bust out in songs of praise to him.
The Lord protects his people and gives victory.
Psalms 28:6-8 TLB

STRONGHOLDS BROKEN

**Bite the dust, satan, we know who you are
You rotten terrorizer of children
Harmer of innocent people, the lowest
You take your hands off God's child!
We're here to claim her back in Jesus' name!**

**Your strongholds are being broken, with God's authority!
We take her back by force
With the WORD! The BLOOD! And The NAME OF JESUS!
We bind you with all three!
We stake you out of reach of her
We break the assignments of those under you
We set your prisoner free in Jesus' name!
We cover her with a blanket of Christ's blood!
We fill her with the living Word of God!
We protect her with the name of JESUS!
In Jesus' name we set her free!!**

That at the name of Jesus
every knee shall bow in heaven and on earth and under the earth,
and every tongue shall confess that Jesus Christ is Lord,
to the glory of God the Father.
Philippians 2:10-11 TLB

Take the sword of the Spirit, which is the word of God.
Ephesians 6:17 TLB

And they overcame him by the blood of the Lamb.
Re 12:11 TLB

DOWN, DOWN, DOWN

She was swirling down, down, down
Being pulled down by some
Force, she thought was
Uncontrollable
Down, down
Down
When
Suddenly
She remembered!
She was in charge!
The force had no right
It was she who had the authority!
She arose as was her right!
She fought with the Blood!
She spoke the Name,
Everyone knew!
Jesus, Jesus
Jesus!
down
down
down
went
the
evil
force
Of course!

❖ ❖ ❖

Because of this, God raised him up to the heights of heaven and gave
him a name that is above every other name.
Philippians 2:9 NLT

BOW, NOW!

**At the name of
JESUS
Every knee has to bow
In Heaven and earth
And under the earth
Every name
Must come under the authority
Of the name of JESUS!
The evil one
And all his demons
Large and small
Sickness and disease
Hopelessness
Fear and discouragement
Hate and unrest
Bitterness and despair
Unforgiveness
Unwantedness
Unlovelyness
All of these
Lies!
So, bow now!
And come
Under the
Authority
Of the
Name of
The
LORD
JESUS CHRIST!**

...So that that at the name of Jesus every knee will bow,
in heaven and on earth and under the earth, and
very tongue will confess that Jesus Christ is Lord,
to the glory of the Father. Philippians 2:10-11 TLB

DEMONS RISING IN THE NIGHT

Demons rising in the night
Causing us such fright
Get out of here in Jesus' name!
Remember this is why He came!

Demons rising in the night
Causing us such fright
You're nothing but wisps of air!
You've been conquered in Jesus' name!

Demons rising in the night
We're watching as you fade from sight
You can never live in His light!
Jesus is King! Bow your knees!

Demons gone in the night
Demons replaced by His light
Gone is the fear, replaced by His peace
As we bow our knees in JESUS' NAME!

Therefore God has highly exalted him and bestowed on Him
the name which is above every name, that at THE NAME OF JESUS
EVERY KNEE SHOULD BOW
in heaven and on earth and under the earth,
and every tongue confess that Jesus Christ is Lord,
to the glory of God the Father
Philippians 2:9-11 RSV

THE WALL OF BLOOD

By the Power and Authority given me
In the name of the Lord Jesus Christ!
To which every knee must bow!

I raise up a wall of blood
The BLOOD of JESUS!
Life saving, cleansing, healing, protecting
BLOOD OF JESUS!

I position this wall of blood
Around my family
And in-between them
And the spirits of influence
That would try to come between
My family and the destiny God has called them to!

In Jesus' name and by His authority
I bind my family's feet
To the paths God has ordained for them
Thank You for Your Word, Father!
And Your peace and love
Over this family of Yours

Finally, let the mighty strength of the Lord make you strong.
Put on all the armor that God gives,
so you can defend yourself against the devil's tricks.
We are not fighting against humans.
We are fighting against forces and authorities
and against rulers of darkness and powers in the spiritual world.
So put on all the armor that God gives.
Then when that evil day comes, you will be able to defend yourself.
And when the battle is over, you will still be standing firm.
Ephesians 6: 10-13 CEV

THE BATTLEFIELD

What about our thoughts, Father?
They flit to and fro; no one knows them but You and I
How can they make such a difference in our lives?
What can we do with our thoughts, Father?
You say, "Cast down imaginations and everything
That exalteth itself against the Knowledge of God" You say-
"Capture <u>every</u> <u>thought</u> and bring it under obedience to You"

It all seems impossible, how do we do this?
Again You say, "Think on things that are true
Things that are honest, that are just, that are pure
Things that are lovely, things of good report
Think on the fine, good things in others
Think about all the things you can praise Me for"

So the way I see it, Father, You're saying
Interrupt and cast down bad thoughts in Jesus' name
Turn our thoughts and our faces toward You

Dear Father, help us to continually cleanse our minds
Washing them in the water of Your Word
Blessed Holy Spirit, stand guard over our thoughts,
Gently sorting them, showing us the right and wrong,
The good from the bad
Lord Jesus, continue to teach us how to fight these battles
With Your Word, Your Name, Your Blood
Thank You that You will do this for us, Father

For the weapons of our warfare are not carnal,
but mighty through God to the pulling down of strongholds
Casting down imaginations, and every high thing that exalteth itself
against the knowledge of God, and bringing into captivity every
thought to the obedience of Christ. 2 Corinthians 10:4-6 KJV

BATTLE LOST

I fought the fight
But my heart was wrong
I judged and scorned
The ones who wouldn't stand with me
And to my sadness, I saw
A look of misery on their faces
As they saw the enemy whip on me
Now that I've blown the battle
And made a fool of myself
Please show me, Father
What is Your way for me

Child, the idea was right
But the attitude was wrong
If you're going to lead the way
You must look into My face
You must walk in My grace
You must lead in love or you'll be disgraced
It is not by your might or strength
You are not better because
I've given you eyes to see
I've chosen you to be a leader
Leaders lead in love
So that those who come behind
Can watch and see and recognize Me

And if I have the gift of prophecy, and know all mysteries
and all knowledge; and if I have all faith,
so as to remove mountains, but have not love, I am nothing.
1 Corinthians 13:2 NLT

LIFT US, FATHER, SO WE CAN SEE

Father, You are a Great and Mighty God
Lord of the heavens and earth, Lord of the sea
Oh, Father, lift me high and hold me up so I can see
I want to see things like You see them, through Your eyes
Eyes of Love, love that comes from Your heart
I want to see Your Truth, so it can set me free

Father, raise up Your believers into an army
An army carrying the banner of Your truths
Endowed with Your Power, that comes from above
Because You are the truth that sets men free

Oh Father, open our eyes and let us see
Teach us how to have the victory
Father, we carry Your Word to the lost and bound
It is Your truth that binds the enemy
And sets Your people free

Father, help us to understand that in us, is Your greatness
We want to sing Your battle cry, Victory! Victory!
Freedom to the bound, life to the dying, love to the unloved
Oh Father, lift us high
Hold us in Your arms so we can see
Please, please, please

The precepts of the Lord are right, rejoicing the heart; the
commandments of the Lord is pure and
bright, enlightening the eyes. Psalms 19:8 TAB

YOUNG WARRIOR

Dear Warrior - in - training, child given by God Himself
Sent here to learn to serve your King
He put me here to train you up, to plant the precious seeds
To stand guard with you, as we watch these
seeds sprout and grow
To call down the Spirit Wind to blow,
To call the Son of God to warm them
To ask our Father God to send rain
To teach you how to pull the weeds, to teach you
how to fight the fight
To teach you how to serve your King
Dear young warrior - the seeds are growing
It's time for you to take up your position
To stand firm and guard these seeds
You will need to grow them strong and tall
Large enough to feed and train and supply
The family the King will be giving you
Put on your armor, young warrior; pick up your weapons
The WORD, the NAME, the BLOOD
Stand guard over what the King has given you
I'm proud of you, young warrior
Great warrior man - I see you just ahead
Strapped in your armor, weapons in place
Standing guard over yours
And all that belongs to your King
Showing people the way, leading them to freedom
Planting the seeds of truth, guarding them as they grow
Great warrior man, take my hand as we stand guard together
Over what belongs to our King

They will be mighty warriors for God,
grinding their enemies' faces into the dust beneath their feet.
The Lord is with them as they fight; their enemy is doomed.
Zachariah 10:5 TLB

WARRIOR IN TRAINING

Child, you spend so much time worrying
About not being able to stand
Let Me tell you one more time
You will never be strong enough to stand alone
You will always have to rely on My strength
The problem isn't that satan is too strong
The problem is that you remove yourself from My strength
You do this with your words of distrust, with your fears
There will always be these fears and lack of trust
Little arrows aimed at you from the enemy
You must bring them to Me immediately
Do not roll them over and over in your mind
Do not concentrate on them
It leads to worry which is useless
And gives satan a mighty foothold
It can even give him a victory on the battlefield of your life
Take up your weapons, child; you are a warrior in training
I will be inside you, over you, and around you
I will be watching you, guiding you, leading you
The only time you will get into trouble
Is when you wander away from Me
Then instead of seeing Me, you see fear
Fear opens the door to the enemy as faith opens the door to Me
Take My hand, pick up your shield of faith
Put your eyes on My face, remember I'm training you
I love you, child; I did not pick you to do something
That I wouldn't give you My strength and power to do

Finally, be strong in the Lord, and in the strength of His might. Put on the full armor of God, that you may be able to stand firm against the scemes of the devil. Ephesians 6:10-11 NAS

ASK FOR GOD'S POWER!

Child, come bow down before Me
The time has come for Me to anoint you
From this time forth My power will flow through you
As you touch others, it will be Me touching them
As you pray for the sick, it will be Me Who heals them
As you fight the demons, it will be Me fighting them
As you bind the spirits, it will be with My power
As you loose My Spirit, it will be Me flowing into them

How I love you, child, I love you so much!
Child, you have not, because you ask not!
There are so many things to be done
Ask! Set Me free to move on behalf of your people
Your town, your world, your life
My power abides in you, child; use it

Now glory be to God who by his mighty
power at work within us is able to do far
more than we would ever dare to ask or even
dream of--infinitely beyond our highest
prayers, desires, thoughts, or hopes.
Ephesians 3:20 TLB

He Made Everything Beautiful In It's Time.
He Has Planted Eternity
In Men's Hearts And Minds
(A Divinely Implanted Sense Of Purpose
Working Through The Ages Which Nothing
Under The Sun But God
Can Satisfy).
Ecclesiastes 3:11 TAB

THE END THAT'S ONLY THE BEGINNING

ALL THINGS WORK TOGETHER

Dear Father God
I just want to tell you *thank you*
Thank you for my life
From my beginning day, to this day
And for every day that is to come
There are things I wish had never happened
And things I hope to never have to face
There have been the good and wonderful times
Love and happiness, joy and peace
I want to take this opportunity to *thank You*
For never leaving me or forsaking me
For walking with me
Through the good and the bad times
I just want You to know that I'm beginning to understand
That nothing has ever happened to me
That You have not allowed to happen
Each and everything has had a purpose
And I stand on the Word that says
All things will work together for my good
Because I love you so much

And we know that all that happens to us is working for our
good if we love God and are fitting into his plans.
Romans 8:28 TLB

NOTHING IS IMPOSSIBLE

Nothing is impossible
For I have settled in my mind
That my Father Jehovah
Will take care of me

So I will sing to the Lord
As I rise from my bed
I will praise His name
As I return to the same
For all the days and years of my life
Nothing will be impossible

For His strength and love are mine
His loving kindness covers me
He hides me in His secret place
Blessed be the Name of the Lord

Let everything everywhere bless the Lord.
And How I bless him too. Psalms 103:22 TLB

SHINE THROUGH ME, FATHER

Father, a new day is here
The sun is shining brightly
Across the lake the reflections are crystal clear
It makes me think about You and I
How when I look into Your eyes
I can see myself reflected
I don't see the person I think I am
With my faults and shortcomings
I see my reflection crystal clear
Covered by Your Son's precious blood
Father please help me to carry this picture of myself
Help me to remember that I can only be
The person You want me to be
When I let YOU shine through me

Now this Lord is the Spirit, and where the Spirit of the Lord is, there
is freedom. And we with our unveiled faces reflecting like mirrors
the brightness of the Lord, all grow brighter and brighter as we are
turned into the image that we reflect; this is the work of the Lord
who is the Spirit.
II Corinthians 3:17-18 Jerusalem Bible

NEW BEGINNINGS

New beginnings, how do they come about?
They are new every morning, every noon and night
New beginnings begin every time you look into the Father's face
Every time you say, "I'm sorry, I really want to do it Your way"

Thank You, Father, that over and over we get to start again
Thank You, Lord, thank You from the bottom of my heart
Thank You, Father, that when satan tries to slay us
You step in and hold us while we prepare to start again
You lift us up and dust us off, give us a hug
You say, "This is the way, walk here, child"
Thank You for new beginnings daily in our lives
Thank You, Lord, that You are all-knowing, all-seeing, all-loving
Thank You, Father, that You are everything to me

The Lord's loving kindness indeed never ceases
for His compassions never fail.
They are new every morning; great is Thy faithfulness
Lamentations 3:22-23 NASV

THE STEADY THREAD

Life is made up of many things
The good and the not so good
There are the hurts
And the joys
Which hold such blessings
The fears and discouragements
The hopes and prayers

The unending
Hours of whys and wonderment
The searching
And the finding
The failures and the changes
The challenges and the overcoming
More hurts, more joys, more life

But through it all there runs a thread
A strong steady thread
Sewn there by The Mighty One
As it weaves its way through our lives
It brings help in the hard times
An encouragement and strength
Unknown to us

THE END THAT'S ONLY THE BEGINNING

A calmness in the uncalm times
Forgiveness for the unforgivable
Love when we think we can't love
A beautiful thread of peace, joy, and security

This thread is sewn by the very hand of God
To draw us closer and closer to Himself
Weaving in, weaving out
As we experience the joy of knowing we are one with Him

Does the God who lavishly provides you
with his own presence,
his Holy Spirit, working things in your lives
you could never do for yourselves,
does he do these things
because of your strenuous moral striving
or because you trust him to do them in you?
Don't these things happen among you
just as they happened with Abraham?
He believed God, and the act of belief
was turned into a life that was right with God.
Galatians 3:5-6 The Message

THE OLD NOTEBOOK

Today I found an old notebook
From it seems like long ago
As I read the pages
I was sad for the goals unfulfilled
I grieved and felt like giving up

As I reread and rethought
I realized that although
I may not have reached those exact goals
What I have learned is precious to me!

I've learned many wonderful ways of
Talking and listening to my Father
How to pray unceasingly
To stand on The Word and pray it back to Him
To Pray in faith not fear!
How to let go of the past, how to forgive

And when I look through my Bibles
They look well worn and loved
With signs of many hours spent in my Fathers presence
Then I think of how I've learned to sit at His feet
Resting my head against Him
Hearing Him say, "This is where the weary come to rest"

I think the enemy wants me to look at myself
As an undisciplined failure
As he points to my lack of self-control
My unorganization
And screams, "You blew it!"
My head starts to hang

Then from the center of my being
Comes the Whisper
"Well done good and faithful servant!
This is what I want from you
That you should sit even closer to Me
Take My hand child and look into My face
Don't listen to him!"
For I have great and mighty things to show you!

Now glory be to God who by his mighty power within us
is able to do far more than we would ever dare to ask or even dream
of—infinitely beyond our highest prayers, desires, thoughts, or hopes.
May he be given glory forever and ever through endless ages
because of his master plan of salvation for the church
through Jesus Christ. Ephesians 3:20, 21 TLB

THROUGHOUT ETERNITY

I bow down before You, my King of kings
I sit at Your feet, my Father God
I reach up and touch Your face
And I am overwhelmed
By Your great love for me

You hold out Your arms to me
As we dance and twirl together
Through the long corridors of eternity
Moving and swaying to unending songs of praise

I know what it's like to hear
Your soft whispers of truth
As we dance on and on and on----without end!

He made everything beautiful in its time.
He has planted eternity in men's hearts and minds
[a divinely implanted sense of purpose working through
the ages which nothing under the sun but God can satisfy].
Ecclesiastes 3:11 TAB

This was His plan from all eternity, and it has now
been carried out through Christ Jesus out Lord.
II Timothy 1:9

GIVING THANKS ALWAYS

As you can see the thread of thanks giving runs through this book page after page. As I stood watching my house burn down. And then four months later hearing our boat had sunk in the icy Alaska waters, knowing that my husband only had a few minuets of survival time in the cold water. When I heard this horrible news, the Holy Sprit surged up from the center of my being, all I wanted to do was drop on my knees and sing praises and give thanks to my Heavenly Father. Not because my house had burned, or that my husband was quite possibly dead, but because my God was in control, He could see everything, He knew exactly what was going on and He had promised to take care of things. His Word said that He would work all things out for my good. Now was not the time to question, but the time to thank Him! And in doing so to completely trust Him with my life, no matter what was happening. To make a bad story good, my husband of 54 years, and his crew were all rescued in time. The Lord replaced our home with a much nicer one, and our fishing boat with a bigger and better one, in time for the next fishing season. I thanked Him for allowing me to learn these major thanks-giving lessons, but I told Him I didn't think I needed to practice any more on the big ones.

It's a good idea to start out on the small things, a thank you here and a thank you there. As I lay in bed with my grandchildren we practice saying thank you prayers--no asking tonight, only thanking. How thankful the Father must be when we do this, and how thankful we learn to be also.

To give thanks is really not a choice, but a command. So as with everything, the sooner we start the better off we will be, and His peace we will receive as He promised.

Following is a list of Bible verses about giving thanks, (only a part of what's in Gods Word). Please read them and give the Blessed Holy Spirit a chance to show you the importance of giving thanks to our Great Father God. It is the desire of His heart that we do so.

Always give thanks for everything to our God and Father in the name of our Lord Jesus Christ. Ephesians 5:20 TLB

No matter what happens, always be thankful for this is God's will for you who belong to Christ Jesus. 1 Thessalonians 5:18 TLB

GIVE THANKS SCRIPTURES

For this I will give thanks and extol You, O Lord, among the nations; I will sing praises to Your name. 2 Samuel 22:50 TAB

Give thanks to the LORD, call on his name; make known among the nations what he has done. 1 Chronicles 16:8 NIV

O give thanks to the Lord, for He is good; for His mercy and loving-kindness endure forever! 1 Chronicles 16:34 TAB

Now, *our God, we give you thanks,* and praise your glorious name. 1 Chronicles 29:13 NIV

The trumpeters and singers performed together in unison to praise and *give thanks to the LORD.* Accompanied by trumpets, cymbals, and other instruments, they raised their voices and praised the LORD with these words: "He is so good! His faithful love endures forever!" At that moment a cloud filled the Temple of the LORD. 2 Chronicles 5:13 NLT

After consulting the leaders of the people, the king appointed singers to walk ahead of the army, singing to the LORD and praising him for his holy splendor. *This is what they sang: "Give thanks to the LORD; his faithful love endures forever!"* 2 Chronicles 20:21 NLT

Then he restored the altar of the LORD and sacrificed peace offerings and *thanksgiving offerings* on it. He also encouraged the people of Judah to worship the LORD, the God of Israel. 2 Chronicles 33:15 NLT

They sang antiphonally praise and *thanksgiving to GOD:* Yes! GOD is good! Oh yes--he'll never quit loving Israel! All the people boomed out hurrahs, praising GOD as the foundation of The Temple of GOD was laid. Ezra 3:11 The Message

195

At the dedication of the wall of Jerusalem, the Levites were sought out from where they lived and were brought to Jerusalem to celebrate joyfully the dedication *with songs of thanksgiving* and with the music of cymbals, harps and lyres. Nehemiah 12:27 NIV

For in the days of David and Asaph of old, there was a chief of singers and *songs of* praise and *thanksgiving to God.* Nehemiah 12:46 TAB

I will give thanks to the LORD because of his righteousness and will sing praise to the name of the LORD Most High. Psalms 7:17 NIV

I will give thanks to the LORD with all my heart; I will tell of all Your wonders. Psalms 9:1 NASB

Therefore will I give thanks and extol You, O Lord, among the nations, and sing praises to Your name. Psalms 18:49 TAB

That I may make the voice of thanksgiving heard and may tell of all Your wondrous works. Psalms 26:7 TAB

The LORD is my strength, my shield from every danger. I trust in him with all my heart. He helps me, and my heart is filled with joy. *I burst out in songs of thanksgiving.* Psalms 28:7 NLT

The LORD is my strength and my shield; my heart trusts in him, and I am helped. *My heart leaps for joy and I will give thanks to him in song.* Psalms 28:7 NIV

Sing to the Lord, O you saints of His, and *give thanks at the remembrance of His holy name.* Psalms 30:4 TAB

To the end that my tongue and my heart and everything glorious within me may sing praise to You and not be silent. *O Lord my God, I will give thanks to You forever.* Psalms 30:12 TAB

Give thanks to the LORD with the lyre; Sing praises to Him with a harp of ten strings. Psalms 33:2 NASB

GIVE THANKS SCRIPTURES

I will give you thanks in the great assembly; among throngs of people I will praise you. Psalms 35:18 NIV

These things I remember as I pour out my soul: how I used to go with the with multitude, leading the procession to the house of God, *shouts of joy and thanksgiving among the festive throng.* Psalms 42:4 NIV

In God we have made our boast all the day long, and *we will give thanks to Your name forever.* Selah [pause, and calmly think of that]! Psalms 44:8 TAB

I will make Your name to be remembered in all generations*; therefore shall the people praise and give You thanks forever and ever.* Psalms 45:17 TAB

Offer to God the sacrifice of thanksgiving, and pay your vows to the Most High. Psalms 50:14 TAB

I will give You thanks forever, because You have done it, And I will wait on Your name, for it is good, in the presence of Your godly ones. Psalms 52:9 NASB

Willingly I will sacrifice to You; *I will give thanks to Your name,* O LORD, for it is good. Psalms 54:6 NASB

He who brings an offering of praise and thanksgiving honors and glorifies Me; and he who orders his way aright [who prepares the way that I may show him], to him I will demonstrate the salvation of God. Psalms 50:23 TAB

Bless our God, O peoples, give Him grateful thanks and make the voice of His praise be heard. Psalms 66:8 TAB

Let the peoples praise You [turn away from their idols] *and give thanks to You, O God; let all the peoples praise and give thanks to You.* Psalms 67:3 TAB

I will praise the name of God with a song *and will magnify Him with thanksgiving,* Psalms 69:30 TAB

We give praise and thanks to You, O God, we praise and give thanks; Your wondrous works declare that Your Name is near and they who invoke Your Name rehearse Your wonders. Psalms 75:1 TAB

So we Your people and the sheep of Your pasture Will give thanks to You forever; To all generations we will tell of Your praise. Psalms 79:13 NASB

I will give thanks to You, O Lord my God, with all my heart, And will glorify Your name forever. Psalms 86:12 NASB

What a beautiful thing, GOD, to give thanks, to sing an anthem to you, the High God! Psalms 92:1 The Message

Let us come before His presence with thanksgiving; let us make a joyful noise to Him with songs of praise! Psalms 95:2 TAB

So, God's people, shout praise to GOD, *Give thanks to our Holy God!* Psalms 97:12 The Message

Enter his gates with thanksgiving and his courts with praise; give thanks to him and praise his name. Psalms 100:4 NIV

Give thanks to the LORD and proclaim his greatness. Let the whole world know what he has done. Psalms 105:1 NLT

Praise the LORD! *Give thanks to the LORD, for he is good!* His faithful love endures forever. Psalms 106:1 NLT

Deliver us, O Lord our God, and gather us from among the nations, *that we may give thanks to Your holy name* and glory in praising You. Psalms 106:47 TAB

Oh give thanks to the LORD, for He is good, For His loving kindness is everlasting. Psalms 107:1 NASB

Let them give thanks to the LORD for his unfailing love and his wonderful deeds for men. Psalms 107:15 NIV

Offer thanksgiving sacrifices, tell the world what he's done--sing it out! Psalms 107:22 The Message

But I will give repeated thanks to the LORD, praising him to everyone. Psalms 109:30 NLT

With my mouth I will give thanks abundantly to the LORD; And in the midst of many I will praise Him. Psalms 109:30 NASB

PRAISE THE Lord! (Hallelujah!) *I will praise and give thanks to the Lord with my whole heart in the council of the upright and in the congregation.*
Psalms 111:1 TAB

I will offer you a sacrifice of thanksgiving and call on the name of the LORD. Psalms 116:17 NLT

I will confess, praise, and give thanks to You, for You have heard and answered me; and You have become my Salvation and Deliverer. Psalms 118:21 TAB

Open to me the gates of righteousness; I shall enter through them, *I shall give thanks to the LORD.* Psalms 118:19 NASB

You are my God and I will confess, praise, and give thanks to You; You are my God, I will extol You. Psalms 118:28 TAB

O give thanks to the Lord, for He is good; for His mercy and loving-kindness endure forever. Psalms 118:29 TAB

My lips shall pour forth praise [with thanksgiving and renewed trust] when You teach me Your statutes. Psalms 119:171 TAB

At midnight I rise to give you thanks for your righteous laws. Psalms 119:62 NIV

All the people of Israel--the LORD'S people--make their pilgrimage here. *They come to give thanks to the name of the LORD as the law requires.*
Psalms 122:4 NLT

Give thanks to him who alone does mighty miracles. His faithful love endures forever. Psalms 136:4 NLT

Give thanks to him who made the heavenly lights-- His faithful love endures forever. Psalms 136:7 NLT

Give thanks to him who parted the Red Sea. His faithful love endures forever. Psalms 136:13 NLT

Give thanks to him who led his people through the wilderness. His faithful love endures forever. Psalms 136:16 NLT

I will give You thanks with all my heart; I will sing praises to You before the gods. Psalms 138:1 NASB

I bow before your holy Temple as I worship. *I will give thanks to your name for your unfailing love and faithfulness, because your promises are backed by all the honor of your name.*
Psalms 138:2 NLT

Every king in all the earth will give you thanks, O LORD, for all of them will hear your words. Psalms 138:4 NLT

I will give thanks to You, for I am fearfully and wonderfully made; Wonderful are Your works, And my soul knows it very well.
Psalms 139:14 NASB

Bring my life out of prison, that I may confess, praise, and give thanks to Your name; the righteous will surround me and crown themselves because of me, for You will deal bountifully with me.
Psalms 142:7 TAB

All Your works shall give thanks to You, O LORD, And Your godly ones shall bless You. Psalms 145:10 NASB

Sing to GOD a thanksgiving hymn, play music on your instruments to God,
Psalms 147:7 The Message

AND IN that day you will say, I will give thanks to You, O Lord; for though You were angry with me, Your anger has turned away, and You comfort me. Isaiah 12:1 TAB

LORD, You are my God; I will exalt You, *I will give thanks to Your name;* For You have worked wonders, plans formed long ago, with perfect faithfulness. Isaiah 25:1 NASB

"It is the living who give thanks to You, as I do today; A father tells his sons about Your faithfulness. Isaiah 38:19 NASB

The LORD will comfort Israel again and make her deserts blossom. Her barren wilderness will become as beautiful as Eden--the garden of the LORD. Joy and gladness will be found there. *Lovely songs of thanksgiving will fill the air.* Isaiah 51:3 NLT

Thanksgivings will pour out of the windows; laughter will spill through the doors. Things will get better and better. Depression days are over. They'll thrive, they'll flourish. The days of contempt will be over. Jeremiah 30:19 The Message

[There shall be heard again] the voice of joy and the voice of gladness, the voice of the bridegroom and the voice of the bride, *the voices of those who sing as they bring sacrifices of thanksgiving into the house of the Lord, Give praise and thanks to the Lord of hosts,* for the Lord is good; for His mercy and kindness and steadfast love endure forever! For I will cause the captivity of the land to be reversed and return to be as it was at first, says the Lord. Jeremiah 33:11 TAB

But I, with a song of thanksgiving, will sacrifice to you. What I have vowed I will make good. Salvation comes from the LORD."
Jonah 2:9 NIV

And they had a few small fish; *and when He had praised God and given thanks and asked Him to bless them [*to their use], He ordered that these also should be set before [them]. Mark 8:7 TAB

He also took a cup [of the juice of grapes], *and when He had given thanks,* He gave [it] to them, and they all drank of it. Mark 14:23 TAB

Profound and reverent fear seized them all, and they began to recognize God and praise and give thanks, saying, a great Prophet has appeared among us! And God has visited His people [in order to help and care for and provide for them]! Luke 7:16 TAB

Then Jesus was filled with the joy of the Holy Spirit and said, *"O Father, Lord of heaven and earth, thank you for hiding the truth from those who think themselves so wise and clever, and for revealing it to the childlike.* Yes, Father, it pleased you to do it this way.
Luke 10:11 NLT

Was there no one found to return and to recognize and give thanks and praise to God except this alien? Luke 17:18 AMP

Because when they knew and recognized Him as God, they did not honor and glorify Him as God or give Him thanks. But instead they became futile and godless in their thinking [with vain imaginings, foolish reasoning, and stupid speculations] and their senseless minds were darkened.
Romans 1:21 TAB

Those who have a special day for worshiping the Lord are trying to honor him. *Those who eat all kinds of food do so to honor the Lord, since they give thanks to God before eating. And those who won't eat everything also want to please the Lord and give thanks to God.*
Romans 14:6 NL

I always thank God for you because of his grace given you in Christ Jesus.
1 Corinthians 1:4

But thanks be to God, who gives us the victory [making us conquerors] through our Lord Jesus Christ. 1 Corinthians 15:57 TAB

While you also cooperate by your prayers for us [helping and laboring together with us]. *Thus [the lips of] many persons [turned toward God will eventually] give thanks on our behalf for the grace (the blessing of deliverance) granted us at the request of the many who have prayed.*
2 Corinthians 1:11 TAB

All of these things are for your benefit. *And as God's grace brings more and more people to Christ, there will be great thanksgiving,* and God will receive more and more glory. 2 Corinthians 4:25 NLT

Yes, you will be enriched so that you can give even more generously. *And when we take your gifts to those who need them, they will break out in thanksgiving to God.* 2 Corinthians 9:11 NLT

Carrying out this social relief work involves far more than helping meet the bare needs of poor Christians. *It also produces abundant and bountiful thanksgivings to God.*
2 Corinthians 9:12 The Message

Nor should there be obscenity, foolish talk or coarse joking, which are out of place, but rather thanksgiving. Ephesians 5:4 NIV

Though some tongues just love the taste of gossip, Christians have better uses for language than that. Don't talk dirty or silly. That kind of talk doesn't fit our style. Thanksgiving is our dialect.
Ephesians 5:4 The Message

And you will always give thanks for everything to God the Father in the name of our Lord Jesus Christ. Ephesians 5:20 NLT

Every time I think of you, I give thanks to my God.
Philippians 1:3 NLT

Do not fret or have any anxiety about anything, but in every circumstance and in everything, by prayer and petition (definite requests), with thanksgiving, continue to make your wants known to God.
Philippians 4:6 TLB

Our prayers for you are always spilling over into thanksgivings. We can't quit thanking God our Father and Jesus our Messiah for you!
Colossians 1:3 The Message

Let your roots grow down into him and draw up nourishment from him, so you will grow in faith, strong and vigorous in the truth you were taught. *Let your lives overflow with thanksgiving for all he has done.*
Colossians 2:7 NLT

You're deeply rooted in him. You're well constructed upon him. You know your way around the faith. Now do what you've been taught. School's out; quit studying the subject and start living it*! And let your living spill over into thanksgiving.* Colossians 2:7 The Message

Be earnest and unwearied and steadfast in your prayer [life], being [both] alert and intent in [your praying] with thanksgiving.
Colossians 4:2 TAB

Thank [God] in everything [no matter what the circumstances may be, be thankful and give thanks], for this is the will of God for you [who are] in Christ Jesus [the Revealer and Mediator of that will].
1 Thessalonians 5:18 TAB

In everything give thanks; for this is God's will for you in Christ Jesus.
1 Thessalonians 5:18 NASB

GIVE THANKS SCRIPTURES

I urge you, first of all, to pray for all people. *As you make your requests, plead for God's mercy upon them, and give thanks.* 1 Timothy 2:1 NLT

Through Him then, let us continually offer up a sacrifice of praise to God, that is, the fruit of lips that give thanks to His name. Hebrews 13:15 NASB

They said, "Amen! Blessing and glory and wisdom and thanksgiving and honor and power and strength belong to our God forever and forever. Amen!" Revelation 7:12 NLT

And they said, "We give thanks to you, Lord God Almighty, the one who is and who always was, for now you have assumed your great power and have begun to reign. Revelation 11:17 NLT

Available on Amazon.com, CreateSpace.com, in Kindle format, and other book and online retailers.

Made in the USA
San Bernardino, CA
21 August 2017